I0407825

Cancer Kills the Caregiver, Too

BY

KIMBERLY BRATTON
VIXEN PUBLISHING

Kimberly Bratton

Vixen Publishing

Kimberly Bratton

Cancer Kills the Caregiver, Too

Plus

The Caregiver's Guide to Survival

COPYRIGHT

Vixen Publishing

Contact Information

Kimberly Bratton

Email us at: vixenpublishing@yahoo.com

Cover Image: Courtesy of Pixabay

Dedication

I dedicate this book; *Cancer Kills the Caregiver, Too*, to many people. First, to my deceased mother, Linda Helton who fought the arduous battle with breast cancer twice in her lifetime and she did it with courage and dignity. She passed away five years ago and I miss her every single day.

I would also like to dedicate this to my beloved aunt, Sharon. She is battling her own cancer now and my Uncle Larry is her caregiver. You are a brave and very strong woman Sharon and you are in the best of hands. Have faith.

Lastly, to my husband Gregory, who was diagnosed with cancer four years ago. It has been a long and difficult fight but he3 is in remission now and God willing, he will stay there. I am his caregiver and our journey through cancer was my inspiration to write this book.

To all the caregivers of the world:
Stay strong and know that you are not alone.

Kimberly Bratton

Table of Contents

Kimberly Bratton

Introduction

"Cancer sucks!" There's no other way to say it. Cancer cuts you off at the knees and never looks back. It doesn't care who you are or how much money you have. It doesn't discriminate when it chooses its victim. It only wants to destroy and destroy it does.

Few words in the dictionary can send that instantaneous chill of fear down your spine like the word "Cancer." As soon as you hear it, it changes you forever. Some will fight it while others will shrink away from it. Some patients will survive it and some will not. Regardless of how cancer plays out in the life of a patient and his loved ones - no one gets away from the devastating and sometimes deadly effects of what that word actually means.

Fighting cancer is the hardest thing anyone will ever do. I have seen it with my own eyes. For those who have fought and survived, I commend you. It takes great courage and strength to win this particular battle. Cancer is not for the weak-hearted. It takes every ounce of strength someone has to fight it. But it also takes bravery, willingness to fight and a strong desire for life. They say attitude is half the battle, they are right. A cancer patient has to want to win the fight for life in order to battle this deadly disease.

Those who make through the darkness know that cancer, even cured, never leaves you. It remains in your heart and in your head and even in your body, as the devastating treatments you underwent are evident to anyone with eyes.

This book is not meant to take anything away from the cancer patient but hopefully it will shine some light on a person who works so hard for the patient: the caregiver.

Cancer definitely changes the person afflicted but it also changes everyone around that person. Cancer is never satisfied to take just the patient. It wants to kill the life around the patient, too. And it begins with the person who is the patient's next line of defense, the Caregiver.

In this book, *"Cancer Kills the Caregiver, Too,"* we will explore the caregiver's role in cancer, how they struggle, and how they persevere. I wrote this book to recognize those who take care of the sick every day. Being the primary caregiver for a terminally ill patient is draining, scary and often intimidating as you are being asked to do things you probably have never done before; such as flushing ports and giving injections.

For most caregivers, being a nurse will become second nature. The hard part will be the persistent loneliness and isolation the caregiver feels when eventually everyone disappears and they are left alone with the patient. I call these brave people, "The Forgotten Ones," caregivers lost in the shuffle.

They do all the work, taking on every role; nurse, doctor, cook, mother, father and maid yet they receive the least amount of attention or care. Oftentimes, they are left weakened from neglect and the grief they carry in their hearts every day, a grief they can't allow the world to see. They try to be strong for the patient and for everyone else; but who is strong for them?

Being the caregiver of a terminally ill person is almost as hard as being the patient. Some would say it can be harder. While the patient is being taken care of, the caregiver has to be everything, all at the same time and usually for extended periods of time; some times for years.

Caregivers need care too; otherwise, there could be a second patient somewhere down the line.

Whether cancer has come for you or a loved one, be assured, it alters your universe. When the doctor first told me that my husband had cancer, I could feel as the fibers of my life began to unraveled. Walking back to our car, I felt so heavy from the weight of it that with each step I took I expected a crack to form in the ground beneath me and swallow me whole.

Cancer afflicts every part of your life and the lives of those around you. It devastates your relationships, your job and finances, your social life and some of the time, it takes your life.

The caregiver is there at the center of it. They are forced to experience every unpleasant moment while picking up the slack and somehow, miraculously, they make it all work.

I know first-hand what it is like to be a caregiver. My husband has Multiple Myeloma. He has been receiving treatment for four years. We have spent many long days and nights at the Cancer Center or the hospital. If I had to guess, I would say that I have spent a years' worth of days there - waiting on him to return from one procedure or another.

During the long periods lingering in hospital corridors, I saw so many men and women, caregivers who were just like me, all going through similar sorrows. At first, I only noticed their shadows. I didn't see the people but I knew they were there. I was seeing the world through dazed, almost catatonic eyes.

But after a few months the fog began to fade and I began to notice that I was seeing the same people over and over again and suddenly I realized that I was one of many.

Mostly, we came in pairs: the cancer patient and a caregiver. You could tell the newbie because of the hope, fear, and tears in their eyes and you could tell the ones who were all too familiar with the process because their eyes were glued to IPads and Smart-Phones. For me, it was a laptop and a Blackberry that saved me from the boredom and tedium that would otherwise have driven me insane

The Cancer Center is the last place I would've thought it possible to make any solid, lasting friendships; but that was the case for a small group of us. We bonded over our shared experiences and it made us feel, somehow, not so alone.

We would schedule doctor visits on the last Friday of the month so we could gather and chat while our patients moved from appointment to appointment.

These became counseling session for us in a way and I think I can speak for us all when I say, they were also very comforting.

We would talk about our frustrations and how tough it is sometimes to get our patients to cooperate. We talked about insurance or lack thereof and we shared information about assistance programs and charity's. Mostly, we just vented about everything.

I began to notice that I was hearing the same things from each of them. Certainly, we all had our own challenges but we all had some common anxieties; like where to turn for help and who to trust. Sometimes hospitals staff were not all that

knowledgeable and if you got a particularly
ignorant one, they can even be detrimental.
Therefore, knowing where to turn for information
becomes a necessity and I realized, other
caregivers where the best ones to ask. They have
been through it all, they know the ropes, and their
brains are full of valuable information. Find a
caregiver buddy, one with experience and it will
help you more than you will ever know.

We learn from others and that is what this
book is for. Hopefully as you read it you will find
some useful, but most importantly, comforting
words to help you as you proceed along this
unpredictable and heartbreaking journey.

No one will ever understand how hard it is
to be a caregiver, but I am afraid more will. The
data I see indicates that cancer will afflict every
one of us in our lifetimes, one way or another. As
cancer claims more victims; it makes more

caregivers. Though these brave groups of people have been left out up to now, there will certainly be more interest placed on them as their numbers continue to grow.

Cancer is never a pretty story and it doesn't always have a happy ending but we need to know that we, as caregivers, are not alone. There are many out there like us. You can form your own local groups, chat rooms or websites but find other people sharing your experience and the loneliness that you are feeling right now will diminish somewhat. Sharing builds caring and we all just want to be cared about. Isn't that right?

I asked my caregiver friends if they would be willing to share their experiences with cancer, the ups and downs, the joyous times, and everything in between. To my delight, they agreed.

Their names are Lola, Marcus, and Beatrix and their stories make up Part One of "*Cancer Kills the Caregiver, Too.*" When you read each of them, remember that these could be anyone's stories: you, me, or someone we love.

I want to thank Lola, Marcus, and Beatrix for your inspiration and courage. I know many people will see themselves in your stories and hopefully, your strength will give them strength to get through the hard times.

Part Two of this book, *"The Caregivers Guide to Survival"* and is a valuable resource for all things "caregiver". I have been a caregiver multiple times in my life. I have learned and grown with each experience. These times of caring for someone else has given me a unique perspective on the subject and an expertise that I would've preferred not to have. I sincerely hope that you can benefit from this unwanted knowledge of mine.

I want to thank you for spending your time reading it and when you are done I hope that you will pass it on to someone who could also benefit from it. Good Luck and Godspeed. .

Kimberly Bratton
1/15/2017

Disclaimer: I have changed some names to protect the privacy of those involved.

Part One

Life Stories

Marcus and Karen

"Denial became my friend, and then it became my enemy." Marcus

The rug was pulled out from under our quiet little world when Karen came to me and said she needed to go to the hospital. I was surprised to hear her say that because Karen has always hated hospitals and refused to go unless it was life or death. Her mother and father both died in hospitals when she was very young and even today, the sterile smell of a hospital room makes her want to faint.

I inquired as to what was wrong. My Karen was never one to complain about anything so this caught me off guard.

Then Karen told me that she had been feeling bad for months, if not longer and she had ignored it for as long as she could. That was Karen's one and only fault. She was a head-in-the-sand type person and it often took a baseball bat upside the head to make her acknowledge that an issue had arisen. This trait of hers came from living with alcoholic parents; she learned early that oftentimes it was better to ignore things than to deal with them head on. I never realized it until now but Karen has sometimes lives in denial, too.

But now the symptoms were worsening and she was alarmed, but instead of going to the hospital, we went to her primary care doctor. After a thorough examination, he sent Karen directly to the hospital with possible gall bladder involvement.

After four days in the hospital and an unknown number of tests, a small group of doctors appeared at Karen's door. They told us who they were and what their specialties were, but honestly,

I don't remember a single one of them. Their faces were just a blur to me.

They began throwing out all kinds of words that meant nothing at the time. Then the gastroenterologist in the group told us that based on the initial exam, they had all concluded that Karen's gall bladder needed to come out. So they sent us home to wait for a call to schedule surgery.

So it's only a gall bladder, no big deal. We can handle that. They take it out and life goes on as usual.

Once at home, Karen ate a cheese sandwich then went on to bed. She was exhausted and slept for the better part of two days.

When Karen finally got up from her considerable slumber, she said her stomach was hurting and went to the bathroom. I was in the kitchen making her some soup when I heard her yell my name. The panic in her voice sent panic through me as I ran down the hall to my wife.

When I opened the door you would've thought I'd walked into a horror movie. Karen was vomiting blood, so much blood. It was on the wall and the floor. It ran down the front of her gown.

My darling wife looked at me with fear in her eyes as she vomited again and again. I had never seen so much blood. I got a washcloth and held it under cold water, then began dabbing her sweating forehead with it. When the violent vomiting stopped, I got her off the floor, cleaned her up, and dressed her. Within minutes, we were in the car heading to the hospital again.

The hospital was not far from our house but before we could get there, Karen cried out that she was going to vomit again. I reached for a quart jar that I kept in the car to throw loose change into, emptied the coins on the back floor, and handed it to her just in time. Karen filled the jar, we stopped to empty it in a dumpster, and then she filled it again before we made it to the hospital.

I carried my wife into the emergency room, sat her down, and went to check her in. The lady at the desk told us to have a seat; it may be a while before she is seen. The emergency room was filled to capacity that day.

After sitting for a mere thirty minutes, without any warning Karen began retching but before I could get the trash can, she threw up blood all over the floor in the waiting room. Patients screamed in horror while others scurried as fast as they could to get away. They immediately put Karen in a room and there we waited.

The nurses came and went. They took her vitals and gave her medicine to stop the vomiting, and then they took her for more tests.

I waited for over an hour in that stifling room when a young man came in to tell me they were admitting Karen into the hospital. He gave me some forms to sign then took me to my wife.

She was lying in the bed when I arrived, curled up in a fetal position; she looked so small and frail and was sleeping soundly. I kissed her forehead then sat down beside her.

She slept for a long time and I dozed off as well. A while later I was awoken by a gentle hand on my shoulder and a quiet voice asking if I could come to the hall for a minute. I left Karen's room and was met with a team of doctors who informed me that they were taking Karen in for exploratory surgery right away. They needed to place an endoscope down her throat to look inside her stomach. With that much blood, they were expecting to find a bleeding ulcer.

So now we have gone from gall bladder to a bleeding ulcer. I felt good that in some small way that had to be a blessing.

The surgery took a couple of hours and in that time I watched a bit of TV and eventually dozed off. I woke up when they brought Karen back in. She looked pale and lifeless and in some way that renewed my fear from earlier but never once did I expect Karen to do anything but recover completely. She had a tennis tournament coming up next week and nothing could make her miss that, not even illness.

When Karen began to wake she was disoriented. She couldn't remember much of what happened and maybe that was a good thing. She asked me what was wrong with her but I wasn't able to answer many of her questions. I told her we had to wait for the doctors but that I felt sure we would be going home soon. I promised to take her out to dinner as soon as we got out of the hospital. Karen chuckled a bit and then to my astonishment she said that we would not be going out to eat anytime soon. I asked her what she meant by that and she told me that she was going to die.

I was speechless. What would make her say such a thing?

A little while later, one of the doctors came in and explained that the blood was indeed coming from a bleeding ulcer and that she'd apparently had the ulcer for some time. He told me they repaired it and she should be well enough to go home the next day to prepare for the gall bladder surgery. Then he told me to go on home and get some rest because the drugs they were giving her would keep her out all night.

I asked the doctor why he was still doing surgery if the bleeding ulcer was the problem. As he was rushing out the door, he informed me that the ulcer was an additional complication not "the problem." Then he was gone without allowing me any more questions.

I took his advice and went home to find the mess in the bathroom that I had forgotten about. It took hours to clean up the dried blood and by the time I was done, I only had enough energy left to make a sandwich, grab a beer, and sit alone in front of the TV. I fell asleep in my recliner and didn't wake until the phone rang the next morning. It was Karen. She was extremely upset and asked me to come right away.

I arrived within the hour and when I walked into my wife's private room, I was aghast at the sight of her. Her skin and eyes were extremely yellowed and the nurse told me this was jaundice. It had started during the early morning hours. Then she told me this could still be caused by the gall bladder but they were looking into liver issues as well.

They took her for an MRI and then performed an ultrasound on her abdomen. That was when they discovered a bile duct blockage caused by two tumors. The blockages would not allow the bile to pass from the liver to the intestines thus causing the extreme jaundice. It became imperative that they reroute the bile immediately so they took Karen back into surgery.

I didn't understand much of what they were saying and honesty I didn't really want to know. I just wanted them to fix Karen.

When my wife of 40 years returned to me she had a tube exiting the upper part of her abdomen and entering just below and to the right of her naval. It was a horrible sight. I was glad Karen was still asleep because I didn't want her to see the horror on my face. Being severely yellowed, lifeless and now with an artificial object protruding from her, she looked so pitiful to me. I couldn't let her see that.

The nurse explained it to me as best she could to say that the tube allowed the bile to be carried from the liver to the small intestine, bypassing the gall bladder and bile duct. I asked the nurse how long Karen would have to have that horrendous tubing coming from her body? Was there any way we could get it removed before Karen ever saw it? The nurse looked at me with a mixture of empathy and sadness as she told me the doctor would be in soon. She then handed me a few pamphlets and suggested I read through them while I waited for the doctor. I laid them on the chair next to me and I sat there feeling shock and disbelief.

When the doctor finally arrived Karen was just waking up. He asked if I had looked over the material the nurse left me and I shook my head no. This seemed to irritate the doctor somewhat but he went on to explain that things were worse than we initially thought.

There was a complete blockage of the bile duct by two distinct tumors. The good news was that Karen's gall bladder was fine and would not need to be removed but the bad news was that these tumors could not be removed either. They had grown around the arteries and to remove them would likely kill her on the table.

It was then that Karen felt or sensed something unfamiliar and lifted her gown to expose the artificial tubing protruding from her abdomen. The look of horror on her face broke my heart and when the doctor told her she would have that in for months, if not longer, she began to cry. I told the doctor about the tennis tournament coming up and how was she going to play with that thing coming out of her. He looked at us both in turn, shook his head, and declared that there would be no more tennis for Karen, at least not for a very long time.

Karen was now in the fight of her life, we just didn't know it yet, and I refused to believe that our life was going to change, especially for the worst.

I inquired as to their course of action and he informed me that they would do chemo-therapy to shrink the tumors in the hopes that they may be operable at a later date. Then he told us not to get to hopeful but to look on the bright side. If Karen's ulcer had not started bleeding when it did, they may not have found the tumors until it was too late.

A nurse came in to give Karen a sedative and before long she was drifting off again. The doctor continued to explain the events but by then my brain had shut down. It was too much to absorb all at once. The doctor handed me a stack of lab reports and various other paperwork. I laid them on the seat next to me. The stack was growing quickly.

Karen fell asleep with a tear on her cheek. I brushed it away, and then went to get coffee.

Walking back to Karen's room, my cell phone rang. It was my sister, Ruth. She had gotten my message that Karen was in the hospital and wanted to know everything. Talking to her made me realize I actually had very little information to give her. I had not processed any of it yet. I told her about the bleeding ulcer and the subsequent jaundice. She asked about the surgeries and had they given me a diagnosis yet. I told her they said there were two tumors that were inoperable but that they were going to do chemo-therapy to shrink them. My sister then asked me what kind of cancer Karen had and at what stage was she?

I was taken aback by her question because no one had even used the word cancer, not once in all the conversations we'd had. I assured her that Karen did not have cancer. We were dealing with a couple of tumors and the doctors were going to get rid of them. That was all.

Ruth listened compassionately as I insisted it wasn't cancer. It began to anger me when she questioned me further, as if her words would somehow give Karen cancer. I know it doesn't work that way but I wasn't thinking rationally at the time.

Karen and I were never blessed with children and she was all I had in the world. I wasn't about to allow cancer in our life no matter how many times Ruth said the word. So I banished all thoughts of cancer from my mind and refused to listen to anyone who thought differently. If none of the nurses, doctors, or technicians had called it cancer then it wasn't so. I chose to believe that this was merely a bump in the road for us and it too would pass. I felt I was being pragmatic but in reality, I was in complete and utter denial as to the seriousness of Karen's condition. Everyone knew it but me.

My sister has always been my rock and she always knew when I needed her. This was one of those times. She was at my house when I arrived home that evening from the hospital. We talked for hours and she went over the paperwork with a fine toothed comb. After spending hours on the Internet, Ruth now had a clear understanding of what we were dealing with but she didn't share all of it with me just yet. She knew it would serve no purpose to upset me, so she let me stay in denial as long as I needed.

Ruth stayed at our house for the next five months to help take care of Karen but also to be there for me. She knew I had trouble dealing with the unknown and if truth be told, she was probably there more for me than Karen.

Karen's friends would come by to visit her, bring her flowers and meals for us. They played cards with her and listened when she needed to talk. They all knew the truth and whenever they asked me how she was doing, I would always say the same thing, "My Karen is doing great and will be back on the tennis team next week."

I saw pity in their eyes when they'd hug me and agree that I was probably right. Well, I wasn't right.

I'd taken a leave from work so I could be with Karen at every appointment and chemo-therapy session. I was too afraid not to be there. She went to the infusion center at the Cancer hospital twice a week for her chemo treatments while I remained in denial as to the reason for the chemo-treatments.

Ruth eventually got me to remove the blinders of denial and accept the truth. She finally convinced me that Karen had cancer and as much as I resisted her, the truth sank in. Karen has an inoperable Intrahepatic Bile Duct Carcinoma.

So there it was. Five months after Karen was first diagnosed I could finally accept the truth. My

Karen did indeed have cancer and it was staged at a four.

I wished Ruth had let me stay in my state of denial. It was safer there. Denial was my friend. It helped me cope. Ruth made me see that my denial was not a friend to my wife. Karen needed to talk to me about things. She needed to talk about death and her final arrangements. She needed to know that our will was done and that I was taken care of, too. She needed to know that I was going to be okay. There was so much she wanted to say to me but my denial was preventing her from doing so. For her my denial became the enemy. It separated us, divided us, and if it continued it would conquer us.

By forcing me to face the truth, Ruth had given Karen and me a little more time together. She made me see that my denial was stealing what time Karen and I had left. Karen was going to die from this cancer but before she did, we were able to see wonder and beauty in our last months, weeks, and days together.

Ruth went home and Karen and I spent our time loving each other, no longer worrying about cancer, just enjoying what we could of each and every day.

Stage four progressed quickly and in less than two years of her diagnosis, Cancer took Karen from me. It was the most devastating moment of my life.

Ruth stayed close to be there for me. Karen's death sent me back into denial, and then anger followed by depression, and finally grief lead me to acceptance. Karen and I had spent our entire lives together and now I had to learn to live life without her.

I am an officer of the Military; alert and observant, but I am also a loving husband and that side of me turned into a puddle of pudding as I watched my wife die of cancer. Everything I learned from 20 years of service went out the window. All the determination, strength, resolve, and ability to analyze and execute a plan I used to take for granted, disappeared and all I felt was fear.

I never understood how hard it was to be a caregiver especially for someone you loved so much. It was by far harder than anything I had ever done in the military. At first it wasn't that bad. Karen managed to keep on doing a few things on her own but as time went on the job of caring for her became harder; not only physically, but emotionally too.

Physically, I could do whatever she needed me to do like lift her into the bath or help her to the back porch to watch the sunrise and the deer graze, but emotionally I was falling apart. The helplessness I felt was beyond anything they trained me for in the military. I was at a loss most of the time and there were even times when I felt like Karen's cancer was killing me too. Sometimes, I wish it had.

Today would have been my wife's 65th birthday and to honor our life together, I write this for her. When I was asked to tell our story, I was terrified of reliving it. I was afraid that writing it all down would deliver me into depression again and I didn't want to go back there. I was finally able to get through a day without gut-wrenching heartache and I was glad for that peace but I could hear Karen's voice in my head, insisting I get busy, write it all down so that her death might help another couple going through the same thing.

From the grave, Karen was still giving me her strength and it is for her that I give this to you.

Marcus

Lola and John

**"No one knows the pain of cancer until you
actually live it." Lola**

My name is Lola. I am 57 years old and
currently live in Georgia with my husband John
(age 60) and our teen-aged son. Our home is in a
gated community with lots of oak trees for
shading. A small babbling creek runs behind the
house and we routinely see deer and the occasional
fox as we have morning coffee or tea on the back
porch.

I went to college, earning a Master's Degree
in Architecture and being top in the class, I had no
problem completing the intern requirements and
subsequently passing the Architect Registration
Examination (ARE). I received a job offer from a
firm in Atlanta, Ga. and began working there in
1985, right after graduation. I look back now and

wish I had taken more time off between graduation and working but hindsight is....well you know.

John and I met at his cafe during a bridal shower for one of my co-workers in 1989. We had an instant attraction and he asked me for my phone number before I left that evening.

I was thrilled when he called a week later and we began to see each other regularly. By 1990 we were pretty much exclusive and by 1992, we were married.

We shared a fabulous life, living in downtown Atlanta. We went to parties and nightclubs. We went to plays at the Fox Theatre and ate at five star restaurants. John ran his cafe and I built a promising career at the firm.

People say that John and I live a charmed life where everything seemed to work out the way we wanted it to; but let me tell you, it was hard work, long hours and sometimes breakfast alone but we were determined to have it all. We held high expectations of ourselves and those around us. John's success at the cafe was notable and it quickly became a trendy spot for Atlanta patrons.

My job at the firm was advancing rapidly and I was on track to be one of the youngest Senior Partners in the firm's history when out of the blue I became pregnant with John Junior. He was born in 1998 and instantly became the most important thing in my life.

My pregnancy put a halt to my becoming a Senior Partner but I didn't mind, we were blessed with this new and amazing replica of us.

Right about the time J.J. was born I began to notice a decline in John's overall energy level. It began slowly but seemed to be increasing over time. It became apparent it was time to make an appointment with our family doctor.

They ran routine test but only found two small kidney stones and high blood pressure. So they placed him on medication and sent us home. Within six months we were back again as John's fatigue was worse than ever.

Once again, they found nothing wrong.

Over the next couple of years our family doctor sent John to a variety of specialists including a neurologist, a gastroenterologist, urologist, and god knows how many others but still they could find nothing specific that would be causing his loss of energy and stamina.

Still hoping for answers, John and I agreed he should cycle through the doctors once again.

Maybe they would search a little harder this time and come up with a diagnosis.

Unfortunately, our visits stopped abruptly when we met again with the urologist. That had to be the worst visit in history and the impact it had on John was profound.

This over-weight, nasty little man had the worst bed-side manner I have ever encountered. I would venture to say that he was also the cruelest human being I have ever met. He had absolutely no interest in finding out the facts about John or his condition and for some unknown reason he seemed to dislike John and me. It became apparent that he also felt the need to denigrate John and embarrass us both

The nurse got John to provide a urine sample and then we sat in the exam room for three-quarters of an hour. After a while I began to think they had forgotten about us when the door opens and the doctor walks in.

The nursing staff did no other tests that day and John was not physically examined, but that didn't stop the urologist from forming his expert opinion anyway.

He looked at John's lab report for about thirty seconds, and then tossed it aside. He took a deep breath, and then stretched his arms back behind his head. He interlocked his short chubby fingers - while leaning precariously back on his small swivel stool.

I expected him to topple backwards at any moment but to my utter disappointment, he never did. After watching with amusement at his entertaining feat of balance; I was very sorry when he finally turned his attention to us. I still cringe when I think about it.

This troll-like man bellowed in a deep, gruff tone, "What are you doing here?"

As the horror of those words delivered in such a hateful manner began to sink in, he went on to say, "There's nothing wrong with you! Didn't I tell you that the last time you were here?"

He refused to listen when we tried to explain what John was going through and when he did listen, he dismissed everything we said.

Then without anything to go on he told John that his symptoms were in his head and that he should see a psychiatrist. Then to my absolute shock this so-called professional told us that, "There is nothing wrong with John physically," adding, "There must be something wrong in your marriage causing his symptoms." After telling us to see a marriage counselor, he wrote in John's chart some horrible remarks, which I would see many years later. He wrote that John was crazy, a textbook hypochondriac with an over-bearing, pushy wife.

All of that was determined simply on a urine sample. What an amazing doctor. I wonder if he looks in a mirror and calls himself God. He certainly believes he's God.

However, none of those things were true. John and I have a great marriage. We were deeply in love back then and we have always had the greatest respect for each other. Our little son brought us so much joy and anyone who knew us would tell you that we were the couple who would make it to the end. Our home exuded love and warmth and we were loved by our friends. Who the hell did this doctor think he was to hang such an appalling label on us?

John was deeply upset, as was I. This unprofessional, rude, arrogant doctor took John's serious issues and completely dismissed them. He was highly respected within the community, but our experience with him caused us to be extremely guarded and fearful of doctors for fear of more such disdain.

To make matters worse, those disparaging notes in his John's file followed him from doctor to doctor and eventually they stopped listening to us at all. I never could get them to see that John was too young to be declining so rapidly and that there had to be a legitimate underlying medical condition causing it.

They began to look at us as if we were nuts and they were starting to make us believe we were nuts. They eventually got me to believe that John was a hypochondriac and before long, I began to dismiss the things he said, too. I regret that mistake that to this day.

After many disappointing doctor visits and being told they couldn't find anything wrong with John, we finally gave up and went on with life as best we could. I was working again at the firm while J. J. attended school and life went on while John did his best to ignore his increasingly uncomfortable pain and steady loss of energy. John loved to work outside and tinker with cars, but it became apparent that he didn't have the strength to do those things any longer.

He managed to run the cafe but relied heavily on his staff for most things. Some days he didn't go in at all. The fatigue was beginning to impact his daily routine in a devastating way and for the cyclist who was used to riding fifty miles a week; this was a new low for him. Not only was his medical condition taking a toll on our relationship, it was also taking a dramatic toll on his ability to complete simple tasks. It was devastating for him to have to face the reality that he was losing his quality of life.

We tried to accept our predicament as a new normal but as time went on it became harder and harder to ignore the effects of it.

In 2008, my company had an insurance change and therefore a change in family doctor was required. I wasn't thrilled at first because we'd been with our current doctor for more than ten years but when I met our new younger doctor I began to feel that maybe he'd be able to discover John's mysterious illness when our previous doctor had not.

I had John's medical records faxed to the new doctor and when our first appointment came; we felt like we were ahead of the game.

The usual tests were done again for John's new file and we thought we were off to a speedy diagnosis. The doctor seemed interested and he genuinely listened to John and I lay it out for him. Then with a reassuring smile he promised us that he would find out what the problem was. I liked this man. He was attentive, soft spoken and courteous and we felt good about the visit. For the first time in a long time we had hope.

When the tests came back and the new doctor was unable to make a firm diagnosis; the best he could offer was fibromyalgia. John and I were not happy with that diagnosis because we felt like it was one of those diseases that doctors go to when they can find nothing else. It was a catch-all diagnosis and John felt in his gut that it was wrong. He then demanded to be screened for cancer.

The new doctor argued that he saw nothing in the test results that would indicate cancer and he dismissed the idea entirely. I should never have let him get away with that. We should have pressed him.

If I learned nothing else, I learned that my biggest mistake was in trusting the doctor instead of my own gut feelings. It was a very costly lesson. Doctors are not Gods, no matter how much they want you to believe they are. They sometimes don't listen and they often make mistakes. My advice to you is this: always trust in yourself. It's your body; you know what is normal and what feels out of place better than anyone else.

Another two years crept by with nothing much to show for it. By then, my once strong, healthy, energetic husband had pretty much given up his hobbies, like cycling, woodworking, and tending to our property. He was having a hard time working on vehicles and he was struggling at the cafe. He had relinquished much of his duties to his manager and co-manager. I didn't know until later just how much he was relying on them. I was working, too, and I just assumed John was also.

Before long, John was in constant pain, fatigued and I could tell that his mind wasn't as sharp as it used to be. He would forget things we had talked about and he seemed dazed a lot of the time. John had always been very capable so to see him struggle with simple tasks was not only alarming but also heartbreaking.

I realized how critical the situation had become when I received a call from the co-manager at the cafe. She apologized for calling me but she couldn't reach John and the manager had called in sick.

She had been calling him all morning and she was just about in a panic. I told her to sit tight and I would contact John.

After several unanswered calls, I left work and went home. It wasn't like him not to answer my calls and it was alarming that he wasn't at the café. I mean, he lived at that place.

When I arrived home, I found John sound asleep in bed at one in the afternoon. He was still in his pajamas and his unanswered cell phone was sitting next to the bed. He didn't even hear me come in; he was dead to the world.

I called the cafe and instructed them to close up for the day because John would not be in after all.

I then placed a call to our new doctor and after some insistence; I got John an appointment for the next morning.

I piddled about the house until it was time to pick up J.J. from school. John was still sleeping when his son and I got back home.

We arrived at the doctor's office the following morning and I was determined that we were not leaving that office without a cancer screening. We didn't get one but instead we left with an appointment with an Endocrinologist at the Emory Hospital in Atlanta. That was at least a start. The appointment was in two weeks.

I knew John would not be able to work so I called his sister Emily to run the cafe for a while. After hearing what her brother was going through she gladly agreed to handle everything. Emily is a wonderful sister and part owner of the cafe but right now her concern was for John.

John stayed in bed for most of that two weeks and I took most of it off from work. J.J. went to school as normal and I tried to hide from him just how sick his father really was but J.J. wasn't blind. He knew something was going on.

The Endocrinologist was a very pleasant young woman and we liked her right away. She had a great bedside manner: gentle and caring. After listening to our plight and reviewing his file, this young woman scheduled numerous tests that were done that day. Then she asked us to return in a week for the results.

When we saw her again she informed us that the test indicated that John had Parathyroid Disease. Then she explained what that meant.

Parathyroid glands are glands of the endocrine system which are located in the neck behind the thyroid. There are four of them and they are normally the size of a grain of rice but in some cases, they begin to grow thus introducing enormous amounts of calcium into the body. These extremely small glands control how much calcium is in our bones and how much calcium is in our blood. Since calcium is one of the most important elements in our body and is used to control many systems and organs, the parathyroid glands carefully regulate this process. If they are not functioning properly, it can cause issues all over the body.

She said that in John's case, the parathyroid gland was producing such enormous amounts of calcium that his body couldn't process it. Then she told us that a simple surgery to remove the affected gland would solve all of John's symptoms.

"The treatment is simple." she said. "It would be a short out-patient surgery, then a week recovering at home."

She said that eventually John would wake up in the mornings feeling a little better every day until he was back to living a normal healthy life, doing all the things he loved. I thought: how much better could it get than that?

We left the hospital that day feeling encouraged. It didn't seem like we would ever get an answer, yet a positive one. John has been suffering for the better part of ten years and all he needed was a simple surgery? It seemed almost surreal and by my nature, I was delighted but guarded.

John and I went to the hospital for pre-op testing in preparation for the surgery. It took all day and I sat for most of it in the waiting room drinking coffee and trying to get some work done on my laptop. Thank god for my laptop.

Sometime later, John was returned to me and we were then sent over to the cardiologist for an EKG, but before we got checked in we were called back to the endocrinologist's office.

When we arrived we were quickly escorted to her office and asked if we would like some coffee while we waited. We both declined and the nurse closed the door.

John and I looked at each other and deep inside I could feel impending doom. I could see that John was worried, too. I took his hand as we sat in silence.

When the doctor finally arrived, she apologized profusely for making us wait but what I noticed was the look of concern on her face. Something was wrong.

She told us that during the pre-op testing the x-rays showed multiple lesions located throughout John's body. Somewhat confused I told her that we could deal with those later; right now the parathyroid removal had to come first.

That was when I saw everything on her face. My heart jumped when she said that there would be no surgery because parathyroid disease was not John's problem. Then she uttered those dreaded words that none of us ever expect to hear.

This sweet, caring woman whom we thought was going to be our savior just condemned us with three little words.

John has cancer.

I felt the world shift and all I heard from that point on was those three awful words over and over in my head. I looked at John and immediately wished I hadn't. My heart broke into a million pieces as I watched silent tears running down my husband's cheeks.

We left that day not with a date for surgery but with an appointment with an Oncologist at the Winship Cancer Center across the street. John has Multiple Myeloma and it is terminal in most every case.

That was three years ago and things have ended up much differently than we ever expected. Our lives changed in ways we never saw coming.

John and I are not the same people today. It has been a long, hard road to travel with no sparing of heart-ache along the way. I had no idea what was in store for us once Cancer invaded my husband's blood stream. All I could do was take things one day at a time. With that in mind, I began the whirl-wind ride to hell and back as I spent the first of many days and nights at the Cancer Center in Atlanta.

Cancer didn't just happen to us over-night. It began more than a decade ago, living and thriving in John's body without ever being detected by any of the doctors we had seen. I had never heard of this type of cancer before but now I know more than I ever cared to know it in the first place.

Multiple Myeloma is a cancer that forms in a plasma cell. Plasma cells help you fight infections by making antibodies that recognize and attack germs. Multiple Myeloma cancer cells then accumulate in the bone marrow, where they crowd out and destroy healthy blood cells.

When we first saw the oncologist I had to force them to use the word cancer. For some reason they believe that if they don't say it, then that makes everything okay. It doesn't.

The doctor then told us that during the imaging scans they also found a tumor wrapped around John's spinal cord.

He had been having difficulty getting around but I attributed it to fatigue. But the doctor told us that the tumor was causing his pain during mobility and if left untreated, it would paralyze him within a short period. Therefore, John would have to go through a series of eighteen radiation treatments in order to shrink the tumor.

And so it began, eighteen straight days of making the 40 mile round trip to the hospital for radiation treatments.

On the final treatment of radiation we had our second visit with the oncologist. This visit was by far the worst for me because I asked the question that cancer doctors hate to be asked.

I looked this doctor straight in the eyes and asked him how long John would have had if we had not gotten him to Emory. He tried to tell me that wasn't the point. He said I should be concentrating on what lies ahead. So I asked him again, more firmly this time and when he knew that I was not going to let it go he told us that John had about twelve months but even I could tell he was lying.

I pressed him until he relented and said possibly nine months; no six months and finally he told me that had we not gotten my husband to the clinic John would have died within three months.

My hands flew to my mouth to keep from screaming. Then it all sank in. I would've lost John in three months without treatment and I would have never known why.

Treatment began the next week and the chemo-therapy was devastating to John's body. He managed to endure it for a year and even though it was doing some good, he was nowhere near remission. The doctor told us that John needed to have a stem cell transplant in the coming months or what little progress we had made was for nothing.

John and I spent most of that first year at the hospital and as understanding as my employer was, I had exceeded my available leave. All of my accounts had been turned over to other architects and they were forced to give my lead position to someone else. I tried to go to the office but I was out more than I was there. John was no longer able to stay on his own and since we couldn't afford to hire anyone, the job fell to me. Eventually they fired me. What other choice did they have?

In one day I lost my job and our health insurance. John's treatments were no longer covered and the bills were mounting.

John's sister Emily had filed the paperwork and was able to get John on Social Security Disability within six months. But Disability doesn't come with health insurance. There is a two year waiting period for Medicare.

The hospital agreed to continue treatment but was beginning to become hostile about the enormous size of our bill. They filed for Medicaid and the third time we got it and most of John's back bills were paid.

Then I followed the advice of our social worker at the hospital who told me that because John had a son I could get a disability payment for J.J. too. I did as she advised and we were indeed given a small payment for J.J. each month.

My plan was to use the extra money to pay the hospital what we owed them. I felt better because at least I had a plan now. Medicaid would pay for his treatments and I could get the back bills paid. My plan dissolved within three months.

Medicaid got wind of the extra money coming in and promptly canceled John's insurance because we now exceeded their income limits. This was devastating news to us because John was scheduled to have a stem cell transplant in six weeks and it would cost almost 200,000 dollars.

I drove to the hospital to talk with the Social Worker who gave me such lousy advice and when

I told her they canceled John's Medicaid because of J.J. payments, to my astonishment she said, "Yeah, that sometimes happens." I proceeded to ask her if there was somewhere we could talk privately and she escorted me into the chaplain's office. You can imagine the ass-chewing I gave this woman. I didn't need the check for J.J. but because of it, John's stem cell transplant was no longer covered. Her advice could have cost me my husband.

Like many people, John and I had a small savings account but thinking that we had plenty of time to save more, we had not saved enough. We only had around $25,000. Nowhere near enough and the hospital would not do the procedure without payment. I cried for days because I didn't know what else to do.

They postponed the transplant and kept John on chemo-therapy which cost about $10,000 a month. I paid for the first round of treatment from our savings but was not sure what I was going to do after that. I had to keep what little money we had left for his other medications, which were many and all of J.J. payments were going to the hospital, just to keep them appeased.

The pharmacist that we had used for more than twenty years knew of our dilemma and contacted the manufacturer of the chemo-therapy drug and within a few phone calls we managed to get them to cover the cost of John's treatment until his Medicare kicked in - still many months away.

That was a blessing but things continued to get worse.

Emily had been writing me a check for John's portion of the cafe profits but without John's management skills the cafe was now in the red and closed down that second year. Now there was no income coming in except John's Disability check. J.J.'s check only lasted twelve. This brought about another crisis. I was forced to sell the house or be foreclosed on.

The housing market was in crisis and I wasn't able to get our asking price. The only offer I got was at a tremendous loss so I declined and within three months, the bank foreclosed. We were now living at Emily's house while she stayed with her fiancé.

Things were going from bad to worse and it felt like I was in battle mode every minute of every day. If I wasn't fighting for his treatment, I was fighting for payment.

Collection agencies were calling about past due bills at the cafe and the hospital was calling about past due payments to them. John and I went from financial security to being bankrupt in less than two years because of his cancer.

But John didn't know all the stress I was under because he slept most of the time and I let him sleep. I had read early on that the body fights cancer twice as hard when you are sleeping than it does when you are awake, so even though life for me during those two years was a living hell; John didn't know about much of it. He didn't know my sleepless nights or when I cried for days. He didn't know the isolation I endured or how alone I felt with the weight of the world on my shoulders. I was trying so hard to be strong for him but day-by-day it became harder to handle.

The two year waiting period for Medicare was finally up and the hospital immediately scheduled John's transplant. This transplant is very different than other types as they have to kill John's entire immune system in order to do it.

When I say they took John to death and back is an understatement.

He spent three weeks in the hospital recovering. I spent most of that time with him. I would arrive in the morning and leave at night but most of the time; John didn't even know I was there.

When he as awake he was easily agitated. He would grump at me and even his parents until they finally stopped coming by.

When I got him home, being his caregiver was harder than it had been before. I always had lines to flush and bandages to change but now I had to deal with a deteriorating mind as the newest chemo-therapy drug was slowly destroying his ability to remember anything. I found myself having to repeat things a dozen times and even then it was like talking to a wall. It eventually got to the point where I stopped telling him anything at all, even if it involved J.J.

John struggled with words and found it hard to form sentences. At first I would finish his sentences for him or provide him with the word he was struggling to find; but he became annoyed with me for doing that. I finally stopped finishing his sentences and let him struggle with the words but this made him madder and eventually we stopped talking to each other altogether. It got to where talking to John took too much effort and was never satisfying. I felt like he wasn't listening because he had stopped caring about anything but his cancer.

His parents began to visit again once he was at home from the hospital but he always managed to hurt their feelings with his thoughtless and sometimes cruel words. John's illness also caused irreparable damage to the relationship I had with his family. She would constantly criticize the way I was taking care of him, telling me I wasn't doing enough until finally I lost control and let her have it. She and I have not recovered to this day and likely never will.

Our friends kept away for the most part because, quite frankly, they just didn't know what to say or do. When I would run into them at the supermarket or the bank the very first thing they would say to me was, "How is John?" They never asked about me, nobody did; as if they thought John was the only one who mattered. They didn't come around much so it made them feel better to ask. Just once, I would have loved it if someone, even John, had asked about me.

Cancer patients think only of themselves. I have often said that once they gave John that diagnosis he no longer cared about anything, not life or the cafe, not J.J. not even me. It was now all about him. Cancer patients feel the need to be selfish because they think that is what it takes to survive. But they forget that they are not the only ones condemned to live their nightmare. The ones around them live it as well.

The damage cancer has done to John is measurable by his doctors but the damage it has done to me is immeasurable. Before cancer, John and I had the world by the tail. We were heading for big things. His cafe was thriving and I was a successful architect. We owned our home and had a nice little savings account. We had a marriage that made others envious and for a while, we were happy and healthy. We had a brilliant little son and life couldn't have been any better.

Cancer changed everything.

When John was diagnosed with cancer I was naive as to what that would mean for us and for me.

The relationship between John and me was always one of mutual respect and trust. We always talked everything out and we made decisions together. Before long I was making all the decisions and the weight of that was like having an elephant on my chest.

J.J. was now a teenager and needed his father for guidance as he grew into a man but John wasn't there for him. Because John slept for the better part of two years; my poor J.J. didn't get what he needed and was lost in the shuffle. I don't fault J.J., but my son took full advantage of the new freedom and lack of structure. He knew that his father wasn't strong enough to do anything and he began to act out.

J.J. was belligerent most of the time and refused to do anything I said. He would tell me to get the "hell out of his room," only he used worse language than that. If I didn't leave, he would shove me from the room and slam the door in my face. One time he threw a pencil at me and it struck a mere 1/4 inch from my eyeball. I still have the pencil lead under my skin.

My son was acting this way because his father and I had abandoned him in order to fight cancer. That is my biggest regret of all.

The entire last two years of his high school days were filled with cancer. J.J.'s junior year in high school was hard enough for me but his senior year was a nightmare.

He treated his teachers like he treated me; with disdain. He no longer did his work in class and almost every day I was getting phone calls from teachers telling me that if J.J. didn't begin doing his work, he would fail his senior year.

My J.J. is as smart as they come but unless he is totally engaged in something he enjoys; he puts no effort into it. He was failing most of his classes and he wanted me to allow him to drop-out of school.

Well that wasn't happening. He would graduate if it killed me and it nearly did.

I tried everything. I begged, pleaded, threatened, and rewarded when he actually did something. I even promised him the newest IPhone and possible his own car; but in the end, none of those things worked. It was three weeks before graduation and I didn't know if J.J. would graduate or not. It was an awful feeling to know that I had failed my son so badly.

In the last week of school I was called once again to the counselor's office. They informed me that John Junior managed to bring three of his grades up but his fourth class was still way below a passing grade. Because of this J.J. would not graduate with his class and would have to repeat his senior year. The fate I feared had come to pass.

I began to cry so uncontrollably that the counselor went to get me some water and when she returned; she had J.J.'s teacher in tow. These two women cared a great deal about J.J. and had known him throughout his high school days. They knew that this behavior wasn't typical and wanted to know what was going on. When I managed to get myself under control I did the one and only thing I had left to do. I played the cancer card.

I broke down and told them everything that had happened; the financial ruin, losing my job and the loss of the cafe. I told them we lost our home and were almost penniless. I explained that J.J. had gotten the fuzzy end of the sucker because his mom and dad were forced to place their efforts into saving his dad's life.

By the time I got all this off my chest; these caring women were crying with me. Then they told me to go home and don't worry. They knew how smart John Junior was and were willing to break some rules. They would let John graduate.

That was the one and only time I ever used the cancer card and I hated myself for doing it. But at the time, I saw no other choice. John graduated with his class after all.

To say that cancer is devastating is putting it mildly and I really had no idea the devastation that was in-store for John and me. Cancer kills, that is true, but before it does, it kills everything it possibly can. There is no part of life that cancer doesn't touch but you only learn that the hard way.

I could go on and on about how awful it was; the day-to-day, never-ending chore of being his caregiver. It truly was a test of my strength and in the end, I failed miserably.

We lost our home, all of our money. Cancer stole our love for each other and I lost several years with J.J. as I tended to his father's needs.

I even lost John just not to cancer.

Even though John's cancer is terminal and will kill him one day, he is at least in remission right now, and I am so happy about that but the damage has been done - monetarily, physically, and emotionally. Nothing in our life will ever be the same again.

I lost all pride and I had no sense of self anymore. We had a few friends but none who wanted to be around our sad little world. They all knew us from before cancer and it was hard for them to witness just how far we had fallen. I think they stayed away also because they were afraid that this hell that John and I were living might somehow be contagious - that his cancer might be contagious. They feared the cancer so they feared us. Who could blame them?

For me personally, the worst part was the isolation, not only from John but from the rest of the world. I was alone, struggling to find a way to cope. Enduring John's illness and the occasional verbal abuse when he was sick and out of his mind, were more than I could handle. I sunk into a deep depression. I even wanted to end my own life because I just couldn't take it anymore. All that did was land me in a mental institution.

When I say cancer patients are selfish; nothing drove that home more than a certain triage nurse as I was being admitted to the hospital for severe depression.

During an appointment with my doctor, she became so concerned for my well-being that she ordered me to the hospital by evaluation. When I got to the emergency room I was called in for triage. Across from me sat a young woman who was asking me all kinds of questions about why I was there. I told her that my doctor had sent me over here because I was depressed. Then she asked why I was depressed.

I told her that my husband has terminal cancer and that I have been bearing the burden of being his caregiver for over three years now. Then she asked me if I had ever attempted suicide. I had to be honest with her so I told her about an evening when I was so overwhelmed and took five of my husband's Xanax. Then I made some flippant comment about not waking up in the morning. Of course John knew that five of the pills wouldn't do anything but make me sleep all night, being the smallest dosage made, but J.J. on the other hand became alarmed and called 911.

Within minutes I had a houseful of paramedics and cops. They talked to me for a while, took my vitals, and then asked me to come with them to the hospital. I refused. I knew they couldn't force me as long as I was conscious. I signed some forms then sent them on their way. I slept well that night.

When I told the triage nurse this story she exploded on me. She said, "Why would you do something like that?" I was taken aback by her sudden anger and I didn't know what to say. She then told me she was a breast cancer survivor and that I was a horrible person for doing something like that. Then she admonished me further by saying, "Your husband needs you and all you do is think of yourself? How could you be so selfish?"

I was severely depressed and in emotional pain. I felt like I didn't want to live and this woman, a nurse, blasted me for daring to feel pain. She was the horrible person, not me. You would think that being a cancer survivor herself, likely having a caregiver of her own; she would've had some compassion for me. Instead, she made me feel ashamed even though I knew that I had no reason to be. She made me feel like my needs were of no concern and that I should sacrifice myself to take care of my cancer-ridden husband. She made me feel as if my life didn't matter; only his did. That being said, she proved my hypotheses that cancer patients think of themselves first and everyone else comes second, if at all.

Today, I am on anti-depressants and I see a psychiatrist because I still carry anguish in my heart from everything that happened. John is in remission and getting stronger but I have only just begun to start healing.

I was once a very happy, loving person but cancer dragged me down. I let it beat me for a long time, but now, I am tired of living with cancer. It is time to move on. John and I stay at home most of the time. We have cut ourselves off from family and friends and prefer a life alone with our dogs, cats, and laptops. It is safe, peaceful, and quiet and I think if left alone we can begin to heal from the ordeal we have been through. We have decided to stop living in fear of the next shoe to drop.

John and I have been through so much in our life together and cancer almost destroyed us. But in the end, I know we can regain the feelings we once had, once the trauma has past and the dust has settled.

John and I have won some battles and lost some battles, but we are stronger now than we have been in a long time. Because John's cancer will never completely go away, he will be forever the patient and I, the caregiver. That is our new normal but that's okay because we are still together and I do believe that we always will be. Cancer changed us but it is not going to kill us.

Lola

Beatrix and Carlos

"Trials and tribulations often bring us together." Bea

I was the sole caregiver for my dying husband as he lay stricken with colon cancer. In spite of it all, that last year of his life brought us closer than we had been in a very long time.

Don't get me wrong, it was the hardest time of my life but it was also the best.

Five years ago, life as we knew it came to a screeching halt when my husband of twenty-five years, the father of our three children, was diagnosed with terminal cancer. My name is Beatrix but my friends call me Bea.

Carlos and I have been married for two and a half decades and like some couples, we lead somewhat separate lives. We certainly didn't mean for it to happen, but it did. We began to grow apart. He was working very long hours while I was at home raising the children.

Carlos was driven, successful and he managed to build us an amazing life. Our home was paid for and even though we weren't filthy rich, we had everything we needed or wanted - except time.

Some days Carlos and I only saw each other at meals and bedtime. Sometimes not even that. The boys were consumed with their sports and our daughter, the youngest, was busy dancing her life away in the hopes of being a professional dancer someday. None of us were terribly bothered by the fact that we were all ships that passed in the night. As busy as our lives were, we were all content.

Cancer changed all of that.

I began to notice subtle changes in Carlos's activity level, but considering we were no longer spring chickens, I just chalked it up to age. Little did I know; the cancer had already taken hold of my husband.

Cancer doesn't just appear overnight. It takes many years for it to reveal its ugly head. But once it does, the downward spiral is very fast.

The chemo-therapy treatments are a toxic blend meant to kill the cancer but hopefully not the patient. In my opinion, if the treatment doesn't cure you then it kills you faster than if the cancer was left alone. I know it sounds crazy to think that sometimes it is better not to know.

With his diagnosis came five agonizing years as I watched Carlos go from being an energetic man who loved to play basketball and bicycle with our son to needing my help just to get through the day. Little by little we were losing Carlos and even though we all knew it, not a one of us dared to say the words; at least not in front of Carlos.

He was a man who never gave up and he refused to allow any of us to give up. When he saw one of us descend into sadness, he'd quickly crack a joke to lighten the mood. Carlos could always make us laugh, even when times were really hard and he always saw the light at the end of the tunnel. But he never noticed how dark the tunnel was while he was traveling it.

I knew I had to be brave for Carlos and the children but I also had to be strong for myself. With so much uncertainly flooding our life, I had to make some sense of it fast or cancer was going to kill me too.

It was time to make a choice. I could either see this as being the worst time of my life or make it the best. I chose the latter.

So I followed my husband's lead and put on a happy face. I became determined that cancer was not going to take away what time I had left with the love of my life.

Since the diagnosis, Carlos and I have spent almost every minute together, especially in those last two years. I went to every appointment, test, and support meeting. I took care of him and when he was no longer able to carry on, I picked up the slack. Before I knew it, I became a caregiver, nurse, man of the house and father and mother to our children. Eventually I played every role there was and it was exhausting.

The news we had all be dreading came almost four years to the day of Carlos's diagnosis. I knew it would be coming eventually but the weight of hearing those final words still hurts my heart to this day. We always want to hope things will get better even when we know it won't. I guess that is just human nature.

Carlos and I went to his appointment that day with no real expectation of a change in his condition, good or bad. We had a nice lunch beforehand and we were in a generally good mood. That all changed quickly.

The physician's assistant came to take Carlos for additional blood work, which I found odd because we weren't scheduled at the lab that day. I was taken by a male nurse to the doctor's private office and instructed to wait for Carlos there. The nurse offered me some bottled water which I accepted because I could feel my throat drying out for some reason. Nerves, I suppose.

This entire visit was atypical of any we had been to before.

Two weeks earlier Carlos went through a multitude of physical exams, biopsies, CT and MRI scans, x-rays and labs in order to re-stage his cancer. As these were the same test done every year, I had no real cause for alarm; except something wasn't right. I could feel it. .

When the doctor walked through the door I wasn't happy with the look on his face. We have seen this man every month for four years and I felt like I knew him well. He was not himself that day. He was upset and stressed and that made me extremely nervous.

He sat down in the chair next to me, took a deep breath, and asked if we could talk privately for a moment. I nodded in agreement. He explained that the test results were not good and the cancer had spread to Carlos's liver and lymph nodes. I sat there unable to speak while he detailed the test results for me. I can honestly say that most of what he said never reached my ears but I knew what all this meant.

The doctor saw the anguish on my face then tenderly took my hand, almost like a father would when trying to comfort a child. He said that Carlos would return any minute so if I had questions, now was the time to get them out. I was afraid to ask the question that was circling in my head but I somehow manage to eek it out. I asked this sympathetic doctor how long did we have?

He sighed and with great anguish he said "less than a year."

I slumped back in my chair, dizzy; feeling like the oxygen had been sucked out of the room. I felt time stop as my world came to an utter stand still.

My emotions were spinning in all directions and I thought I might faint. The doctor I have known for four years let go of my hand and returned to his desk as the nurse brought Carlos into the room.

I immediately put on a smile and took Carlos's hand as he sat down beside me.

Carlos looked at me, then at his doctor and he knew. With each word from the doctor Carlos's grip on my hand tightened but being the eternally brave man that he is, he thanked the doctor and we left the office. Still stunned, we made the next appointment, and left the building. We walked in silence to our car, still hand in hand. Then all of a sudden Carlos cursed defiantly and declared that cancer would never get him.

The day-to-day requirements of being a caregiver are demanding and definitely draining, but for some reason, I never felt more alive. I was needed in a way that I had never been needed before.

Carlos and I lived a half century before cancer and that time was very good to us. However, I realize that we took it all for granted, assuming that life would always be the same. Carlos built an amazing business that he would never step foot in again. The cruelty of life with cancer overtook us, it changed everything, and we had to change with it.

I was a loving wife, a caring and attentive mother but for me it was easy to be those things. But something had been nagging at me for most of my adult life. I had yet to discover the reason I was put on this earth. During that last year I came to understand what my purpose really was.

Raising our children to be productive adults was rewarding and I pride myself on keeping a beautiful and warm household. I have friends that love me and I volunteer at the local nursing home twice a week. I ran our children to the moon and back every day and dinner was always on the table when Carlos got home from work. As rewarding as all that was, it was nothing compared to how I felt taking care of Carlos now. I realized that whatever else I might do in my life; nothing would matter more than this. Caring for Carlos in his final days was my purpose in life. Now I understood.

For me, there were no bad days. I began to see everything in a different light. I discovered that most of our grievances in life were petty and it wasn't the end of the world if the Internet went down or the car had a flat tire. The day-to-day inconveniences of life paled in comparison to Carlos's laughter while playing cards or board games with the kids. I began to see the beauty of life and even though I understood that cancer would kill Carlos sooner than later, I wasn't going to let it take him any sooner than it had to. Each day that Carlos woke up was a day of beauty to me.

Some days were more difficult than others, however. As his cancer spread, Carlos became agitated, forgetful and he struggled to find the words he had spoken his entire life. He had given up on caring about anything as he simply waited for cancer to kill him. He even tried to distance himself from us, his family, as if that would somehow make it easier for us to let him go but there was no way I was going to let him get away with that.

As time went on, the days got harder as Carlos was now bed-ridden and his hygiene became my duty too. I could see how this was crushing what little life there was left in Carlos as he watched me take away pee-pots and clean him up. He began to fight me when I needed to flush his ports and soon he refused to take any more medicine. Five years of fighting cancer was finally catching up to him.

He was already in Hospice Care and they were wonderful people, full of love and caring. I called them when I began to hear what many call the "death rattle" as Carlos struggled to breathe. They came immediately and stayed with me and Carlos for the eight remaining hours of his life. They gave him drugs to make it easier but nothing could make it easier for me. I have spent five years being brave and trying to see the positive in our situation but that final day brought the world crashing down on me. I never left his side or let go of his hand. The kids were all there and when the room became oppressively quiet, our beautiful daughter went to her father's side, sat down and kissed his forehead. Then she began to quietly sing to her father. She sang her father's favorite song, "Amazing Grace" and that is when the tears began for me. Carlos took his last breath as she sang the last note. I have never seen anything so beautiful in life.

My Carlos was always a fighter and he fought a good fight - right to the end. We buried Carlos just days before the end of his fifth year of living with cancer.

That last year was harder than the other four combined as I was forced to watch my husband, my best friend, and the love of my life die while I was helpless to stop it.

There were moments of joy, laughter, tenderness in every day but there was also enough pain to kill a horse.

I had conditioned myself to see the beauty rather than the inconveniences and with each passing day I discovered just how wonderful life could be. Yes, cancer took my beloved Carlos, but those final months and years showed me what real love was all about.

I grew up in a Southern Baptist household and we were taught to always be grateful and to show that gratitude every day. I had never thought about Carlos's illness as something to be grateful for, but in the end I realized those years of caring for and loving Carlos were beautiful years and I was grateful to be the one to care for him. Gratitude, love and seeing the beauty instead of the pain became my mantra, one I recommend to every caregiver.

Being a caregiver has gotten a bad name, as most people don't see it for what it really is. Being a caregiver to someone you love can be transcendent, a gift. And yet for too many it feels like punishment.

I concede that I was very fortunate when my husband became ill. We had excellent health insurance and the money Carlos had saved over the years made it possible for me to be at home with him every day and not have the worry of finances. In the end, Carlos had taken great care of me too and now I can take the time to heal without worrying about losing my home or my lifestyle. Carlos was an amazing man and the one true love of my life.

In the early days of Carlos's diagnosis, being a caregiver called for me to be hard as nails as I fought daily for him to get everything he needed. I did tremendous amounts of research on the Internet and I was relentless in making doctors and insurance companies answer my questions.

Being hard-headed with an unwavering willingness to question authority were the tools I had available to use in this fight and I used them to my advantage. It gave me a sense of purpose and it gave Carlos great comfort to know that I was handling everything that he couldn't. It also provided him entertainment as he listened to me on more than a few occasions reading the riot act to some poor insurance rep that had the audacity to tell me that some treatments wouldn't be covered.

I was never an athlete or an entertainer. I didn't know what it felt like for every pitch to be a home-run or every shot a three-pointer. I would never know what it was like to stand on an opening night stage as a crowd thunderously applauds. But I imagine those experiences would pale in comparison to the satisfaction I felt when I was fighting for the man I loved

In the latter days, being Carlos's caregiver meant being there for as many moments as possible. I didn't want to miss anything. My well-meaning friends saw that I was having a hard time and suggested antidepressants or sleeping pills to "take the edge off." Whereas, I certainly understand the desire to do that, I didn't want to be less than 100 percent present; I didn't want to forget a moment.

It is now ten years later and I have become somewhat of an advocate for the caregiver. I went back to finish my Masters and I now have a degree in Psychology. I eventually went to work for the hospital that took such fine care of my dearly departed husband. I counsel caregivers' everyday and I find this as rewarding as I found caring for Carlos.

I pay the bills, keep up our home and I try to be there for our children. I do not intend to ever remarry as there is no one on earth who measures up to my Carlos.

That time spent taking care of Carlos was my meaning of life. It made me stronger than I have ever been and gave me a purpose other than wife and mother. I will never again have that high a purpose. Facing the inevitable death of a loved one changes you in so many ways. It can be a negative experience or it can be positive one. It is all up to you.

Every day I have left on this earth will be spent trying to live up to the person I was in those last years of Carlos's life. His death has taught me how to be a better person. I am not bitter at losing him because I know I will see him again in heaven. Until then, I pride myself on being a little less judgmental, a little more forgiving, a little more generous, and a lot more grateful for the small moments in life. I am a better person for having been Carlos's caregiver. It was his last, most precious gift to me.

Beatrix

Part Two

The Caregiver's Guide to Survival

The Six Letter Word

Cancer doesn't care who you are. It touches people of all ages, races, religions, and incomes. When I was growing up, cancer was a rare creature. It touched only the outskirts of most people's lives. When you heard it, it was always in someone else's family, never your own.

Today, however, that statement doesn't hold true as cancer has become such a common place disease. You only have to visit a cancer ward to see the truth of cancer in the mid 21st Century. At some time in our lives, every one of us will know a person who has cancer and many will have the job of being a caregiver. This book is for the caregiver.

How you approach a cancer patient is different with each patient and their particular cancer. There are no hard and fast rules to follow but I hope this will be a guideline for starting you off on your journey as a caregiver or at the very least, I hope this gives you some comfort as you travel the unfamiliar world of cancer.

The first thing you will want to do is learn as much as you can about your patient's cancer diagnosis. Knowledge is power and in this case, that is particularly true.

For most people, hearing that someone they know has cancer is upsetting. It often makes them think about their own mortality. But death is not always the outcome and for many people with cancer, nearly 14.5 million people in the US today, they deal with their situation as best they can and you must also. This book will help you do that.

In 2016, most cancers are found early as technology has advanced to miraculous levels but that doesn't diminish the fear that comes with a cancer diagnosis.

Some people live with cancer for many years, if not decades but that means learning to live with and adjust to a treatment regimen that can be quite difficult at times. Even though these treatments may save a patient's life, they will permanently change not only the patient but the caregiver, too. Family and friends must also adjust to changes while continuing to provide as much support as possible.

Some patient's never know how long they've actually had cancer. Often there is no clearly identifiable beginning to their illness. Once the diagnosis is revealed and treatment begins, for many, that is the onset and a hopefully, a cure is the outcome.

Those who have survived cancer know that there is always a chance it may come back. They live their lives but the concern is always there.

Cancer is not a diagnosis that comes easily, as in the case of Lola and John. It often takes many visits to the doctor to get a diagnosis. During this time you worry because you have no idea what you are dealing with. All kinds of thoughts go through the patient's mind and through yours. This is a very scary time for all.

Each person's reaction to a cancer diagnosis is a little different but since you know the person you are caring for better than anyone, you will know what is normal and what is not. And you will know how to help them; so be ready. Situations will arise but handle those with patience and love. Sometimes it will be tough but one thing I have learned is that attitude is everything.

Cancer is a disease that can last a very long time and the treatment may continue for many years. At first, people close to the patient are very involved, friends bring you meals and offer whatever support they can. But as the treatment goes on for months or even years, those early supporters may become distant or disappear altogether.

Most caregivers will eventually feel burned out; so don't be afraid to ask for help. The cancer patient needs care almost every minute of every day but you can't be there every minute of every day. Find someone to give you a day off; otherwise, you too, may become a patient.

Remember that your encouragement will give the patient hope and strength to survive the treatments. So, if you're going to be a support person for someone with cancer, plan to hang in there for as long as needed.

And never forget that your patient is a person too. Treat them as you always have; at least as much as the cancer will allow. They will appreciate it and love you for it.

There is a light at the end of the tunnel.

You're a Caregiver. Now What?

A caregiver is defined as the person who most often cares for a person with cancer and is not paid to do so. In most cases, the primary caregiver is a spouse, partner, parent, or an adult child. When family is not available to take on this role then close friends, co-workers, or even neighbors may fill in.

The caregiver has a key role in the patient's care and too often they are not trained for this job. The caregiver is the lifeline of the patient and without them: the patient would have a difficult time at best. Having a good, reliable caregiver is critical for success in the fight against cancer. The emotional and physical support you provide to a person with cancer will be appreciated, sometimes, more than you will ever know.

Cancer has become so widespread that hospitals are no longer able to handle the demands the patients. This prompted the advent of Cancer Treatment Centers in most major cities; allowing treatment to become an outpatient procedure. This now required someone outside the treatment center to be part of the day-to-day care of the patient and as a result, the caregiver was born.

Caregivers wear many hats and these will change as the patient's needs change. Caregivers will serve as nurses, techs, and housekeepers. And eventually the caregiver may even be required to help with the feeding, bathing, and clothing of the patient.

You will schedule appointments, manage insurance issues, keep track of paperwork, and provide transportation. You may even wind up being a legal or financial advocate for the patient if they become unable to perform these tasks alone.

You will be the person the patient leans on and you will become their trusted friend.

You'll also become an important part of the cancer care team. You will keep track of prescriptions and dispense medications. You will watch for and report side effects. You will know which tests need to be scheduled and follow up to make sure that they are. And you will make sure that the patient is being well taken care of by the cancer care team.

Never rely only on the team or their staff to take care of the many tasks involved for your loved one. As we know, sometimes the right hand doesn't know what the left hand is doing. You will need to make certain that everyone is on the same page as far as treatment goes.

.

A good caregiver is a tremendous resource for the cancer care team. In most cases, the caregiver knows everything that is going on with the patient. Make sure you keep a calendar and notes because it is likely that will have to refer back to them at some point.

Your patient will be scared, maybe even a little lost. Be prepared to answer many questions and make it your job to know the answers.

This new job is a going to be a very hard job. I won't lie and sometimes it may feel like you simply have to power-through it. To get through those days you must remember how much your loved one needs you and how much good you are actually doing. You are making a huge difference in the life of one person and with that will come a deep satisfaction. But being a caregiver comes with a cost. Don't allow cancer to kill your spirit or the person you are. Be strong. You are a special person and someone vulnerable needs you.

You will likely be the one to handle everything and this busy schedule can leave you with no time to take care of yourself. This is why it is so important for the caregiver to have someone to count on for support because not a one of us is "super-human."

A caregiver will go through a wide range of emotions while taking care of a cancer patient. A profound sadness comes with having a loved one with cancer. But those like Beatrix may be able to find a personal satisfaction in caring for another person. Bea was able to turn a negative into a positive and she whole-heartedly embraced a new and meaningful role that allowed her to show love and respect for her husband when he needed it most. For her, it felt good to be his caregiver and to know that she was there through it all.

For a nurturing person, the job of caring for someone else can enrich your life in many ways; from a personal satisfaction in knowing you can help someone less fortunate to realizing that you are stronger than you thought you were. What I found most rewarding for myself was the understanding that even in the worst of situations I could step up and do the job; because I was doing it. It bolstered my confidence to know that

Through the process you will definitely find out what you are made of. Being a caregiver requires a deep internal strength and you will learn very quickly whether you have it or not. But you may also find that you have abilities that you didn't know you had, which hopefully will give you a greater sense of purpose and meaning.

The majority of caregivers just do what needs to be done; and unfortunately the caregiver will tend to put the well-being of the patient above their own. You must always take care of yourself, too.

You may think that your love for the patient will get you through this difficult time and hopefully, it will. Still, being a caregiver is a very daunting job. And for many caregivers the commitment is 24 hours a day for months or even years on end.

As the caregiver, you will certainly have an impact on how the patient deals with their illness. The treatment plans are often demanding, exhausting and cause many patients to give up, like my own mother. But with your encouragement and love, hopefully your patient will make it to the end and regain their health.

Being the liaison between the patient and the outside world will also be your job. This can lead to new friendships that can be beneficial to your state of mind. They may even be able to help you along the way with your patient's care.

Caring for someone with cancer is difficult at best, but excelling at it can give you a sense of pride. These good feelings will provide the strength and endurance you need in order to continue in the role for as long as needed.

Being the caregiver can also be painful. People who care for very sick patients may notice their own feelings of sadness and emotional distress developing. They may feel grief over their loved one's illness while feeling overwhelmed trying to manage continuous problems.

Caregivers can develop physical symptoms, like fatigue and trouble sleeping. This is going to be a bigger problem for caregivers who don't take care of themselves or are without a good support system.

There is no planning for an illness like cancer. One day life is normal and the next moment you've been asked to care for a cancer patient. In the blink of an eye; everything changes. This will not be a cake-walk.

There will be times when you know you've done a good job and your patient is doing well. Then there are times when you second guess everything you do and there will be times when you just want to give up, walk away, and not look back. This is all normal and you are not alone.

When you need help, reach out to others, including professionals. Talk with the cancer care team about what you're doing and where you need help. Involve them in your life and your loved one's care.

Talk with a nurse or social worker about services in your area. Talking with other caregivers through organized support groups can help you feel less alone. If you can't visit a support group in person; get on-line. There are communities of people whose lives have been touched by cancer. Through on-line or in person support groups' people share their stories, offer practical advice, and support each other through shared experiences.

Religion can be a source of strength for some people, too. Some members of the clergy are specially trained to help people with cancer and their families. People who are not religious may find spiritual support in other ways like meditation, journaling, or exploring an untapped artistic talent. There are different things you can do and eventually you will feel like you are part of something greater than yourself.

You need to know who you can talk to and count on for help. Families facing cancer can become stronger if everyone takes part in it. Often family and friends want to help but may not know how or what you need. You will have to direct them in most cases. For situations where you need help, make a list. It helps when people can see what you need instead of trying to guess.

Have family meetings to keep everyone informed of the patient's progress. Use these meetings to get some firm commitments from family members to take over so you can get a break. These group meetings are important because people may be more likely to commit under peer pressure. Take advantage of it. Get their names on a calendar. Be very clear about what you need and make sure that the patient is included in all of these meetings.

Someone with young children may not be the best choice for a caregiver. They may be the most loving, caring person on the planet but juggling the schedules of both kids and a cancer patient will be extraordinarily hard.

But unfortunately, many people are forced to do just that. If you fall into this category, you'll need to figure out who will take care of the children while you're taking care of the patient. You may need help from friends and family members in caring for your kids.

There may also be times when the patient's health is compromised and the children cannot be around for fear of spreading germs. You may have to ask other parents, or trusted friends and neighbors to watch your children during these times. It can be a taxing situation on everyone so it is preferable that the caregiver not have young children.

No matter what you do, at some point, you will feel that you've failed in some way. As caregivers, you do the best you can. You try to include the patient, family, and close friends in important discussions and you always have the patient's best interest at heart. But sometime or another you will feel that you could've handled a situation better or done something differently. Guilt may settle in as you second guess every decision. Don't let this happen. You have absolutely no reason to feel guilty. You are doing an amazing thing; you are taking care of someone in need. You are an extraordinary person with a huge heart. Don't let anything or anyone take that away from you. Be proud of what you are doing.

As I stated earlier, being a caregiver is extremely hard and some people are simply not cut out for it. Don't feel ashamed if you are one of these people. It is understandable to feel burdened or even trapped while caring for someone all the time. You may wonder "why me?" You may feel that the caregiver role was dumped on you without your consent. You may feel unprepared or even unable to manage the responsibilities that go with it.

If you became a caregiver because of other people's wishes, you need to really think about how you feel about that and work out those feelings. Mixed feelings at the onset can lead to a greater sense of frustration later on. You should decide on your limits and make them known as soon as you can or the demands of being the caregiver can become a big problem. Addressing potential problems early can help you and the patient get the help you need.

If you really didn't want to be a caregiver but are forced to, it might be helpful to find someone to help you with the job so that you know from the start that the role will be shared. Knowing that you are not alone can go a long way to making the job tolerable and you may find that you are better at being a caregiver than you ever thought you would be.

As a caregiver, you have an important and unique role to fill, likely the most important one of your life. Be proud of the job you do. You are helping your loved one through the worst experience of their life.

Kimberly Bratton

The Patient and the Caregiver

Finding out that someone you love has cancer is complicated. You may have many questions about the cancer and how you should act around this person.

If you are new to the world of cancer then you likely have no idea what is coming so here are a few things you can expect to see from your new patient.

Some common physical changes shared by many people with cancer are listed below. The cancer itself causes some of these while others may be the result of the side effects of cancer treatments. Every patient is different but knowing what to look for will go a long way to making your life as a caregiver much easier to navigate.

Possible Physical Changes

Appetite loss or increase

Hair loss, including eyebrows and eyelashes

Weight loss or weight gain

Extreme fatigue

Changes in taste or smell

Poor concentration or inability to process information - known as chemo brain

Pale skin and lips, or changes in skin color

Problems with sleep

Nausea and vomiting

The toughest side effect to deal with for the majority of cancer patients is fatigue. Extreme exhaustion can become overwhelming and most are caught off guard by just how tired they really do get. And never forget that a cancer patient has a much harder time bouncing back from sickness than the rest of us. Make it a priority to keep them away from sick people, at all cost.

Chemo-therapy treatments are taken for months if not years and often make the symptoms of a cancer patient worsen significantly over time. Add to that the stress of not knowing what your future holds and you can imagine how exhausting that would be for the patient.

Possible emotional changes

Every person will handle the shock of a cancer diagnosis in their own way. Any range of emotions they may have will be normal as a diagnosis brings fear and uncertainty. Emotions become fluid and change from day to day, even hour to hour. You will learn how to handle each of these emotions only by going through them.

Expect all or a combination of the following emotions to occur at one time or another.

Uncertainty

Anger and a sense of being out of control

Sadness

Fear and Frustration

Guilt

Mood swings and intense emotions

Feelings of disconnect or isolation

Loneliness

Resentment

Grief

The effects of cancer and chemo-therapy treatments can be unpredictable. Your patient may feel good one day and not the next, so learn to expect good days and bad days. You must be flexible when living with cancer because no two days are likely the same.

Uncertainty and fear can cause anger and depression, or even withdrawal for the patient. This is normal and is part of the process of grieving for the life that cancer has stolen.

Early in my husband's cancer, I was told by his doctor that it was okay for me to begin grieving. He said, "You are not willing him to die because you grieve for him. It simply gets the process going and makes it easier for you to be stronger at the end." Initially, I found this idea to be appalling but the more I thought about it I came to realize that he could be right.

In the first months of his diagnosis I found myself thinking only of how he was coping and what he was feeling and I didn't stop to think that I was losing something major, too. My life was being stolen as well and it was okay for me to be upset about that. I took this doctor's advice and let my heart begin to grieve and after some time I felt the sorrow fade away, replaced with strength and a new resolve to move forward, to win this battle with cancer or at the very least, I was going to go down fighting like a champion.

Some people are able to adjust to the new reality of cancer in their lives and go forward while others need extra help. Find your local resources and take full advantage of them.

When you are with your patient, show interest and concern; but don't be flippant as this will likely cause the patient to isolate themselves for fear of being dismissed. They want you to be yourself with genuine concern and real conversations not contrived emotions and unrealistic expectations.

Some ideas of conversation starters are below but remember that love comes in many different packages. Express your concern the best way you know how and I promise that your loved one will recognize your feelings and know that you are there for them.

Say anything that comes to mind but sometimes the simplest response is the best. You could say:

"I want you to know I care."

"I'm sorry you are going through this."

"Can I get you a snack?"

"If you would like to talk, I'm here."

"How I can help you today?"

"Do you have errands to run?"

"What would you like to talk about today?"

Most cancer patients are realistic about their disease so don't give them false hope or tell the person with cancer to always stay positive. Don't say to them, "Well, you could outlive me. I could get hit by a bus tomorrow." I know personally that the cancer patient hates that one. It is perceived as being dismissive of the seriousness of their plight.

Try to refrain from saying that you know how they feel or you can imagine what they are feeling. While you can be sympathetic; you can't know how they feel. Only another cancer patient would understand how a cancer patient feels.

It is said that, "laughter is the best medicine" and that it true. When we laugh together - we bond together and when we bond together - we are stronger together. It can be therapeutic and can lift the spirits of everyone around. But it can also be too much sometimes; so take your lead from the patient. If they seem to be getting upset, stop, change the conversation.

There will be days when they don't find anything funny at all and that is normal too. There is nothing funny about vomiting or finding giant clumps of your hair in the hairbrush. Like growing old, cancer is not for the faint of heart. It takes a willingness to fight but on the days when the fight is not there, do not despair. Give your cancer patient some time because tomorrow will bring a new day and a whole new set of challenges.

A cancer patient's appearance will likely change from day-to-day; as one day they may have all their color and feel vibrant and the next day they may be pale and lifeless. If they look good, tell them so but when they look rough, don't bring it to their attention. They are probably aware of it and wouldn't appreciate being reminded of it.

Avoid making comments about weight loss. Whereas most women love to hear the words, "You've lost weight," for a cancer patient, it can be a knife in the heart. During the height of chemo-therapy treatments most patients lose a lot of weight - but what a heck-of-a-way to do it. We all want to be thin and attractive but for the cancer patient, the weight loss is not a good thing. The reality is that they had to knock on death's door to lose the weight and if you point it out, you may not get the response you expect. Rule of thumb: avoid appearance unless they bring it up.

By listening, offering a hand, and giving encouragement along the way you are showing the patient that you want to understand exactly what they are going through. However, being encouraging and supportive of a cancer patient doesn't mean you have to come with pom-poms to make them feel good when they're feeling down. It's important to allow the person with cancer to express their very real feelings of anger, frustration, and sadness. You can encourage them by saying things like, "I'm sorry you're feeling so bad. I can't imagine how you feel, but I am here to listen anytime you need to talk.

In fact, just listening and not talking is probably more helpful than saying the wrong thing. You must listen with your ears and your heart. As one person with cancer put it, "Having cancer go on for years is so debilitating. You need people to get you through it."

Some patients may want you involved with every step of the process and some may not. Some may want to talk about what the doctor said in detail. Others may not want to talk about it at all. Simply asking, "Would you like to talk about it today?" is often all they need in order to open up to you.

When it is time to get test results it is imperative that you are with the patient that day. The process is overwhelming and many times the patient will forget what has been relayed to them. The health-care professionals understand this so don't feel like you are intruding. They want you there in most cases. When the doctor talks with the patient they are really talking to you, the caregiver, so it is important for you to make sure you listen to every word, even record the conversation on your cell phone if you can because the patient will eventually ask you what took place later.

Most doctors will be open about the diagnosis, treatment options, and treatment outlook because an honest approach sets the stage for a trusting relationship among everyone involved. You may find a few doctors that hem-and-haw to avoid your questions and if you have one of these, I sincerely suggest you switch doctors because without honesty right from the start it becomes harder for the patient and support person to trust what is going on. Evasiveness breeds fear.

While talking about the visit with the doctor later you should sense that your loved one is having trouble processing it; take it slow. Don't get into a lot of detail all at once. Let them ask you questions in their own time but be ready to stop if you see them getting upset. Later on, if the discussion is still too much for them, remind the patient that you and the cancer care team are available, concerned, and ready to talk about the illness whenever they are ready.

If on the other hand you find that, you, the caregiver, are having trouble talking about the cancer, you may not be the best person to care for the patient right now. Be honest about how you feel. You may need some time to work through your own feelings before you can help the patient.

Explain to your loved one that you are having trouble talking about the cancer and if discussing the problem with the patient doesn't resolve it, suggest that the patient rely on someone else for a short time. You can suggest that another friend or family member may be better able to provide temporary support and once you have worked out your issues you can resume being the primary caregiver. You can't help someone else unless your own head is on straight. Don't be ashamed as this is more common place than you might imagine. Not everyone is equipped to handle a life and death situation like cancer.

But it's important that you make sure the person with cancer understands that your trouble talking is your issue, not theirs. And don't just leave them hanging; be proactive in finding someone that they can immediately talk with. Also, make certain that the patient knows that your inability to talk about the cancer does not in any way mean that you will not be there for support in the future. Explain that you simply need time to adjust.

Since most people work in some form or another for a living, having cancer brings about other questions; such as, "Should I continue to work?" or "Can I continue to work?"

Working can bring a sense of the importance in a person's life. It can boost the self-esteem and help the patient focus on what they were able to do before they got sick. Work can also be a safe haven and can help bring normalcy back to the patient's life.

The routine and familiarity of a workplace is also a source of stability; a safe place where the patient can encounter other people. Cancer can be isolating, and being around others can be a great source of comfort.

But working is not always feasible. The patient may not be able to perform their job because of the debilitating effects of the cancer thus prompting them to leave their employment. When this happens the patient now has a financial crisis on their hands and the possibility of losing their health insurance.

Cancer's affect on a person's financial situation can be devastating as we saw in the case of Lola and John.

As humans, we tend to live in the moment and unfortunately most haven't made enough preparations for when tragedy does strike. No one should be forced into bankruptcy because they get sick, but for many, that is what happens.

Even if the patient is able to work during treatment they may still face financial problems. The patient may lose pay by being absent from work during and after treatment or the company may reduce their hours anticipating that the patient will not be able to fulfill their obligation to the company. The company may be forced to bring other employees in to do your job and that never turns out well for the person being assisted.

Eventually, if the cancer hangs around long enough, your job will be at risk as well as your financial future.

Any changes in hours worked or pay grade could cause changes in one's health insurance premium. If they work fewer hours or take time off for treatment, you may be required to pay more of your own premiums. In some cases, health coverage may be decreased or stopped completely if the patient is forced into a part-time schedule. A lot depends on your workplace policies. It's important for someone with cancer to understand in advance how schedule changes may affect their insurance, salary, and other benefits.

Frequent medical visits can also be a financial drain because of prescription costs and insurance co-pays. The co-pay is the cost for treatment that the insurance company doesn't pay and is left for the patient to pay out-of-pocket. Co-pays can reach burdensome amounts and in some cases may prevent the patient from seeking further treatment when they can no longer pay the doctors for their services.

There are also traveling expenses to and from the hospital. There are parking fees, gasoline, and the costs of other services and equipment not covered by insurance. The costs add up very quickly. Social Security Disability doesn't always pay enough to live on so the choice to work or not work during your cancer treatment is a tough one and should be thought out carefully.

Being a caregiver can be a full-time job, but many caregivers already have paying jobs and some may have to make the choice between working and being the caregiver.

As with the patient, the caregiver will suffer their own work-related issues; like missed days, low productivity, and work interruptions. Some caregivers may have to turn down promotions or cut back hours. The stress of caring for someone on top of worrying about keeping your job can be overwhelming; however discussing these issues with your boss beforehand can be important for the peace of mind of both the employer and the employee.

There will be times when there will be more demands on the caregiver, for instance, when the patient is diagnosed, getting cancer treatment, getting treatment for recurrence, or nearing the end of life. The employed caregiver may end up having to take a leave of absence from their paying job to be a productive and supportive caregiver. This is when you have to weigh your options very carefully while keeping in mind what is in the best interest of the patient. Sometimes, you have to make tough choices about your life, career, and family when someone close to you becomes stricken with cancer.

For people in certain types of jobs (temps, freelancers, consultants, independent contractors), this is very difficult. If they don't work, they don't get paid. For those with traditional jobs in larger companies, there may be benefits to help you take time off and still keep your job.

When there's no one else to care for the cancer patient, the working caregiver may have to quit their job entirely. If you need to keep your job but the interruptions and time off are creating problems, you might want to look into a different schedule to fit the times your loved one needs you most. You might be able to work half-days or split shifts and some companies even provide paid leave if you are caring for a spouse or close relative.

If you need some time away from work, speak with your boss or benefits office. If your workplace has an Employee Assistance Program, look into what it offers. Some offer counseling services for money issues, stress, and depression. Take advantage of any help you can get.

The Family and Medical Leave Act (FMLA) guarantees up to 12 weeks off per year to take care of a seriously ill family member (spouse, parent, or child). It only applies to larger companies, and not every employee qualifies for it. If you can't or don't want to stop working, you might be able to take unpaid time off under the FMLA.

Keeping your health insurance if you have to quit your job is a major concern. When someone leaves their job, they usually lose their employer's health insurance coverage as well. It's very important for you to have some type of health care coverage. If you're able to pay for your own insurance, COBRA will allow you to be covered for some months after you leave your job. Another option might be applying for insurance from the Health Insurance Marketplace. With the government subsidies currently being provided, you may be able to get good care for less than you might think. Just pick your plan carefully as some have very high deductibles.

Patient Privacy

The privacy of someone's medical records is very important and that is true of a cancer patient as well. If someone you know has cancer, let them be the one to tell others about it. They may want everyone to know or they may not want anyone to know. Whichever, it is their choice to make. You should never share the patient's health with anyone unless you have been given permission.

Often cancer patients need time to process the information before they tell others and may have only shared the news with those closest to them. Others should not take it personally if they are finding out weeks or months later. Instead, focus on how to support that person now that the cat is out of the bag.

Cancer is a scary and burdensome creature. It should never be taken lightly. For the patient, the caregiver, friends, and family - coping with cancer will rank among the hardest things you will ever do.

Coping with Cancer

For most people, when they assume the role of primary caregiver, they do it with the most altruistic of intentions. Everyone likes to think that they will be the best caregiver in history; that they will be patient and loving all the time and that they will always do the right thing. But that is not usually the case. In fact, I would venture to say that even the best of caregivers have a breakdown at one time or another. It seems inevitable to me given the level of stress they endure every single day.

I had a dear friend once named Arthur and he had a lung disease that would eventually take his life. I knew Art and his wife, Susie, for the last ten years of his life and in all that time, Art was ill and Susie was his long-term, sole caregiver.

Susie is exactly the type of person her name implies; she is a petite blond, cheerful, bubbly, and always has a kind word to say. She and Art raised a beautiful son and before Art died, he got to meet his grandson.

I spent a lot of time around Art and Susie and one thing I noticed from the beginning was how patient she always seemed to be. I admired her for being so strong and for giving up her life to care for Art when he needed her the most.

Arthur had been ill for only a short time when I first met them. It would be some years before caregiver stress would show up on Susie.

Art's lung disease was so severe that he couldn't breathe without an oxygen mask; therefore, an oxygen line was installed in each room. They were supplied by a large tank installed in the basement. This gave Art the ability to move around the house and still be safe. I remember stepping over them all the time. They were everywhere.

As the years passed, I began to notice the cracks in Susie's armor as the stress began to build. She seemed to grow angry and somewhat resentful. She loved Arthur with everything in her and took excellent care of him, but looking back, I can see how his illness began to eat away at her. She became a snippy person and she was harsh on many occasions with Art. I was taken aback several times by her callous words and I began to ask myself, "How can Susie be so mean to Art?"

I didn't understand at the time, but I do now. Susie spent her entire life as the wife of a high ranking military officer; well-known and well-respected. She always strove for perfection and she couldn't conceive of disappointing those who held expectations of her. In the past, she never needed to ask for help, she always did everything right, and she made it look so easy. She thought that dealing with Arthur's illness would be just as easy. She was wrong and there were times when I saw her take her frustrations out on Art. Dealing with his illness for so many years eventually changed the person Susie was.

Through the years, I unknowingly watched as Susie changed from the giggly, carefree military wife she was when I first met her to the battle-worn widow I would eventually see sitting at Arthur's funeral.

Arthur saw her suffering, too. On the evening that he died, he told me that he was ready to go. He said he wanted Susie to move on and for me to encourage her to do that quickly. He knew what she'd endured as his caregiver for the better part of two decades and he was now ready to watch her from heaven as she enjoyed the rest of her life. He wanted her days of being a caregiver to be over. "It is her time now." he told me that night. He died a few hours after I left him.

Having cared for other cancer patients and terminally ill people, I have come to realize that no one escapes the stress of being a caregiver. Whether it is due to cancer or some other illness, being a caregiver is one of the hardest jobs and one of the least regarded.

Caregivers are often looked down on as if being a caregiver is just an excuse for not working. Unless you are a caregiver, you don't know the work that goes into being one. The hard work coupled with the stress makes for a volatile combination. Coping with caregiver stress is almost as hard as coping with cancer.

You might begin to notice that you are experiencing feelings somewhat like the person with cancer: disbelief, sadness, uncertainty, anger, and sleeplessness. You may become frightened about your own health and find it harder to concentrate on getting things done.

Learning to recognize the signs of stress can be helpful in preventing bigger issues down the line.

Although every person is different; most will experience one or more of the following during their ordeal with cancer. This applies to the patient as well as the caregiver.

Venting

A stressed-out caregiver may often take their anger and frustration out on those around them. This can be upsetting to family and friends. It may even cause some people to pull back just when they are needed the most. It may help to remember that people often vent their feelings onto those closest to them. They do this because they know that these are safe outlets. They know you'll still be there for them, even if they hurt you in some way now. The patient will do the same thing and they may even take their frustrations out on their caregiver.

Expressing Vulnerability

Sometimes a person with cancer can become timid or passive, looking to others for direction. They seem to resort back to an infantile way of thinking; vulnerable and childlike. This can be very hard for the caregiver.

Feelings of helplessness will often intensify this need to be "taken care of" by the patient. These are normal feelings for a person with a terminal illness to have but for the caregiver this childlike behavior only adds more work for them.

This adds to the frustrations they already deal with daily and could result in health issues for the caregiver.

Harsh Words

A cancer diagnosis and the subsequent treatment phase are usually an uncertain time for everyone; full of anxiety and fear. There's worry about the changes that cancer will bring – financial and job changes, physical and health changes, and even changes in personal relationships.

Because there is so much anxiety all at once, a person with cancer may become easily agitated, upset, or frightened. Fear breeds more fear and soon the caregiver will be feeling equally as frightened and anxious. Sometimes this anxiety will come out as meanness or harsh words either by the patient or the caregiver.

Playing the Blame Game

Sometimes people with cancer blame themselves for getting the disease and sometimes people with cancer blame you for their cancer, as irrational as that may be. If truth be told, not many know where or how they got cancer in the first place, they just did.

As a caregiver, friend, or family member, you may feel guilty about being healthy but don't let it change the way you act toward the person with cancer. You should never feel guilty for something you never had any control of in the first place. It is not your fault or the patient's fault that cancer came along. The important thing now is to get through every day and try to live as normal as possible.

You might ask yourself, "How do I cope with the stress of cancer?"

As different as people are, coping skills are also as varied. What works for one may not work for another. We spend our lives refining our coping skills; learning to manage stress better with each passing crisis. Some people cope best in a privately while others may prefer the group environment. Either way, learning to cope with stress is critical in life and cancer.

One caregiver told me that it was her tendency to be a super-woman and that she often ignored herself in her attempt to "do it all." She would never see the stress building until it was too late; so she solicited her best friend to be her lookout for that behavior.

It worked out well for her. Her friend would let her know when she was coming unglued and she was there to help her regain herself, if needed. Friends need to stick together through this time and have each other's backs. Just knowing someone is there can make all the difference in how you cope with the situation.

Some people find that humor can be a welcome relief from the seriousness of the illness but not everyone will appreciate the humor. Choose your audience carefully.

Be observant during this time because cancer brings a lot of change with it. We have to learn to cope with the changes, be flexible, and adjust quickly. We can't allow ourselves or the patient to become withdrawn and isolated from family and friends. Pay close attention to the mood of your patient; if we feel stress, imagine what they must be feeling.

They are trying to maintain as much control as they can but many will become angry, sad and some may even grieve for the loss of their health and control of their lives. It can be hard for an independent person to be forced to relinquish that control to someone else.

Those with a strong faith find solace in prayer and comfort in their religion. Some people simply choose to remain hopeful and do what they can to guard their hope. Hope may seem elusive a times, but the power of hope is real to those who believe.

Staying positive and optimistic can be excellent medicine for you and the patient. I believe that negative breeds negative; therefore positive breeds positive. Without denying the facts of cancer, try to stay upbeat and encouraging. A positive environment will help the patient feel normal and may save your sanity as well.

If the patient seems nonchalant about the seriousness of their illness, don't assume they're in denial. Talk to them to determine if they need help;

or are they simply trying to cope as best they can. As long as they are attending regular appointments with the doctors, they're probably not in denial. Cancer treatment doesn't afford you the luxury of denial. In the end, it is best to let everyone cope the best way they know how.

How you respond to the difficulties of cancer will affect the way others respond as well. Most people will take their lead from you. Try not to over-react to the changes that take place. Try not to be offended by the harsh words or abusive nature of the patient; remember that they feel like crap most of the time. Try to understand the fear and anxiety that a cancer patient deals with daily. And definitely do not take things personally or you will be upset every minute of every day.

While everyone is adjusting to the cancer it is important to be forgiving, understanding, and supportive. Give the person with cancer time to adjust and make sure that you take the time to adjust also. This is a scary time for everyone but especially for the person facing death. Think about how you would feel if you were in their shoes and take care of them the way you would want them to take care of you.

Cancer is no one's fault and you will need each other now more than ever. It is a good idea to put away hurt feelings from the past and begin fresh because moving forward is the only healthy option to take at this point. Try not to live in the past, but focus on a hopeful tomorrow.

The new responsibilities and worry that come with taking care of someone with cancer is exhausting and the caregiver is not immune to this fatigue. You are so busy caring for the person with cancer that you don't realize how much you are neglecting yourself.

It is time for you to ask, "Who is looking out for me?"

I have a few friends who know me so well that when something is out of sync, they see it before I do. We stay close and they are ready to help at a moment's notice. These are the friends you should have around.

I advise you to close ranks and allow only your chosen friends in the inner circle. Keep them close so that they will see when you are losing it or they can tell you when you are out of bounds or need to re-think something.

You will not be able to do everything and having those around you who can help is more important than anything else, at least for the caregiver. The patient needs love, the caregiver needs help.

There are two ways of coping: healthy and unhealthy. We all have unhealthy ways of coping just don't let them take over when you are feeling stressed and vulnerable. Concentrate on healthy coping and it helps if you know what this means before you need it. Make a list of your strengths, weaknesses, and where you might need extra help. Give the list to those closest to you so they will know what to watch for specifically.

Being a caregiver doesn't mean you have to give up yourself. Find what works for you and stick with it. The American Cancer Society put together the following list of questions in regards to healthy ways of coping. This checklist was adapted from one created by Dr. George Everly Jr. of the University of Maryland. The original appears in the U.S. Public Health Service pamphlet, "What Do You Know About Stress" (DHHS Publication No. PHS79-50097) and is for public use.

Take a moment to look at these questions and answer them honestly. They describe some healthy ways of coping. They'll give you an idea of how well you're holding up, and may help you identify areas where you need to make a few changes in order to take better care of yourself. If you don't already do some of these - or something similar - look for ways you can start working toward those of interest. These small things can strengthen your mind and body and help you make the most of your time as a caregiver.

Answer Yes or No.

1. Do I have supportive family and friends around me?

2. Do I have a hobby or project for work, church, or my community that interest me?

3. Do I have a social life? Do I participate more than once a month?

4. Am I within my weight goal?

5. Do I use relaxation methods like meditation, yoga, or muscle relaxation at least 5 times a week?

6. During an average week, do I get at least 150 minutes of moderate exercise (such as walking or yoga) or 75 minutes of vigorous activity (such as jogging or playing a sport)?

7. Do I eat a well-balanced, healthy meal 2 or 3 times during an average day? (A balanced meal is low in fat and high in vegetables, fruits and whole-grain foods.)

8. Do I make time for me?" Do I do something fun at least once a week?

9.   Do I have a place where I can go to relax or be by myself?

10. Did I attend a support group this week?

If you answered "yes" to most of those then you should be coping well. If you answered "no" to more of them then you answered "yes", then you may need to get some assistance.

Get others to visit the patient to take some pressure off of you. This is a wonderful opportunity for family members to reconnect. Sickness in the family often has a way a creating new beginnings.

But for some people, it will be hard to visit a person who is dying, especially one who looks and feels very sick; it can be shocking and upsetting to see them that way. Sometimes just seeing a lot of medical equipment around someone you care about can be disturbing.

Remind people that this is the same person as always and that they should treat them the same as they always have in the past. Explain that the pleasure you give by visiting them will be appreciated tenfold. Tell them to let the loved one do most of the talking. Being there with kind words, a loving smile, and a soft touch can say a lot more than you could ever imagine to someone who is terminally ill and dying.

Set priorities and manage your time every day. Decide what tasks are most important, how much you can reasonably expect to accomplish and get help where needed. It can be hard to find the time to get everything done but eventually you will find your balance and as a routine emerges, some of the stress will diminish.

Caregiver Depression

Stress and depression in caregivers is very common-place. Dealing with cancer in someone you love is heartbreaking enough but couple that with the pain and suffering, an uncertain future, financial ruin, the constant decisions and battles that come with cancer - well, that all come with a price.

Denial, anger, fear, hopelessness, guilt, confusion, and doubt are just a few of the emotions that cancer brings with it for the caregiver. Whereas it certainly depends on the fortitude of the caregiver; even then it takes a toll. Add a dose of felling helpless to that and you end up with depression.

Depression is horrible for anyone who has it; but it can be a serious health crisis when the caregiver of a sick person suffers from depression. Though not every caregiver will suffer the debilitating illness; most will experience it to some degree.

Depression is not a sign of weakness but rather a sign that something is out of balance. It will not go away miraculously on its own and ignoring these feelings will only make them worse.

Everyone has emotional ups and downs - good days and bad days; but should you notice that you are always sad, have no energy, cry a lot, or easily agitated - then you may be dealing with caregiver depression.

If you are feeling depressed, seek help. Get a friend to give you the day off. Do whatever you like: read a book, watch a funny movie or go for a walk. Remind yourself that there is life outside of being a caregiver and that it is okay to relax and enjoy yourself for however long you can.

You are carrying a heavy burden so it is especially important that you find ways to "decompress."

You may consider some of these:

1. Exercise.
2. Eat healthier.
3. Seek spiritual support, prayer, or meditation.
4. See your friends socially.
5. Do something for you.
6. Plan things that you enjoy.
7. Finish a project.
8. Connect with an old friend.
9. Get your hair and nails done.
10. A massage or a day of pampering.

Most likely, your patient needs a break from the cancer, too. It may be beneficial for you both if you set aside time during the day, like during a meal, when you do not talk about the illness. Talk about the weather, watch the news - or do my favorite - put together a puzzle. Whatever you do, the rule is: not a word about cancer is to be spoken. Normalcy is crucial to the well-being of both the patient and the caregiver. It's a reminder that life does go on.

It's normal to feel overwhelmed by the demands of being a caregiver but if it becomes all-consuming and hinders your ability to function; then you may need to see a mental health professional. If you show any of the following symptoms, seek help right away from a licensed mental health professional.

1. Depressed, physically sick, or hopeless.
2. Desire to hurt yourself or someone else.

3. Hurting or yelling at the people you care for.

4. Using alcohol or recreational drugs heavily.

5. Isolating from your spouse, children, family members, and friends.

6. No longer taking care of yourself or your personal hygiene.

7. No longer showing an interest in anything.

8. Strange or out-of-the-ordinary behavior.

Take depression very seriously and act quickly before it gets worse.

Most caregivers hesitate to relinquish their caregiver duties to someone else, even when they need to for health reasons. They feel that if they take a break, even for a short time - something might happen. In fact, most feel guilty when they do get a moment alone and dare to enjoy it.

Keep in mind that no one can be a caregiver 24 hours a day, 7 days a week, for months or even years on end. Make it a point to get out of the house on a regular basis – even if it's only to shop for food or supplies. This will do wonders to restoring balance and will be recuperative for your body and soul.

Some patients can't be left alone and if you don't have a trusted friend or family member to relieve you, there is another option. You might want to seek help from a respite care facility.

These facilities are described for use as a short-term, temporary reprieve for those who are caring for family members who must be supervised for their health and safety.

Respite gives the caregiver a short break from the exhausting challenges they face every day. It's been shown to dramatically help the caregiver remain healthy and improve their overall sense of well-being.

In most cases, the respite caregiver will come to the home beforehand so everyone can get to know each other before being left alone together. This makes the patient feel more comfortable about being left behind. Remember, no guilt, you deserve this.

The respite care employee will learn the routine, and where everything is kept so that when they arrive for that first visit on their own, they are prepared for anything. They assist the patient with all their needs and are trained to handle most health emergencies. They are the ideal option but they are costly.

Sitter-companion services are another respite option. These are sometimes offered by local civic groups, church or religious groups, and other community organizations. Though not usually professionally trained, these sitter-companion services provide a wonderful low-cost option for respite care; if only for a few hours a day, once or twice a week. Be sure that the sitter-companion knows what to do and who to call - should there be an emergency.

There are advanced respite services located in local facilities where the patient can stay for a few weeks or even a few months. They provide specialized care and are trained for most situations. This gives the caregiver a chance to take a vacation to catch their breath, whether or not they go anywhere.

As the caregiver, you must know your limitations. Don't try to do it all yourself, you are not a super-hero. Being a solo-caregiver is not realistic. Reach out to others. Involve them in the cancer patient's life and in the things you must do for your loved one every single day. When they see how much work it really is, they will pick up some slack.

You know your own body. Be realistic when determining how much you can do. For instance, if you have a bad back don't try to lift the patient alone or catch them when they fall. You may end up seriously injured yourself if you attempt too much.

There are ways you can safely help a person sit up or walk and do it without hurting yourself. A professional physical therapist can teach you how to do these maneuvers safely. They can also assist in getting special equipment, if needed.

Caregivers are often so concerned with caring for their patient's needs that they lose sight of their own well-being. Some of them are so single-minded that they already have one foot over the cliff but they can't see it. And because they can't see it - they will take the next step over, every time.

If it is hard for you to recognize when you are in need and you don't have a trusted friend watching out for you, take this short questionnaire from the American Cancer Society. It was specifically designed to help you determine if you need additional support. This questionnaire can be printed out to take to your primary care doctor for further evaluation, if needed. Make any notes that are pertinent at the bottom.

The questionnaire is reprinted verbatim and can be found on the website for The American Cancer Society. For more information call your American Cancer Society at 1-800-227-2345 or log on at http://www.cancer.org/ for additional information.[1]

---

[1] http://www.cancer.org/

Take a moment to answer the following questions, honestly. Once you have answered the questions, go to the bottom of the page to do a self-evaluation.

During the past week or so, I have...

1. Had trouble keeping my mind on what I was doing..... □ Yes □ No

2. Felt that I couldn't leave my relative alone...... □ Yes □ No

3. Had difficulty making decisions...... □ Yes □ No

4. Felt completely overwhelmed...... □ Yes □ No

5. Felt useful and needed...... □ Yes □ No

6. Felt lonely....... □ Yes □ No

7. Been upset that my relative has changed so much from his/her former self....... □ Yes □ No

8. Felt a loss of privacy and/or personal time.......□ Yes □ No

9. Been edgy or irritable....... □ Yes □ No

10. Had my sleep disturbed because of caring for my relative....... □ Yes □ No

11. Had a crying spell(s)....... □ Yes □ No

12. Felt strained between work and family responsibilities...... □ Yes □ No

13. Had back pain...... □ Yes □ No

14. Felt ill (headaches, stomach problems or common cold)....... □ Yes □ No

15. Been satisfied with the support my family has given me........ □ Yes □ No

16. Found my relatives living situation to be inconvenient or a barrier to caring for them...... □ Yes □ No

17. On a scale of 1 to 10, with 1 being "not stressful" to 10 being "extremely stressful," please rate your current level of stress. _____

18. On a scale of 1 to 10, with 1 being "very healthy" to 10 being "very ill," please rate your current health compared to what it was this time last year. _____

Comments:

(Please feel free to comment or provide feedback if you plan to share this with a health care professional.)

_____

_____

_____

_____

Self-Evaluation

How to determine your score:

1. Count all your "Yes" responses EXCEPT do not count # 5 or 15 yet.

2. Now, look at Questions #5 and 15. If you responded "Yes" to these questions, do NOT count these with your "Yes" count. If you responded "No" to either or both questions, add these to your "Yes" count. (For example, if you had 4 "Yes" answers on the rest of the questions, and you answered "No" to question #5 and "No" to question #15, your total score would be 6.)

Chances are you are experiencing a high degree of distress if you answered "Yes" to either or both questions 4 and 11; or

If your total "Yes" score = 10 or more; or

189

If the score on question 17 is 6 or higher; or

If your score on question 18 is 6 or higher

If you are having a high degree of distress, please don't hesitate. Seek help now.

1. Consider seeing a doctor for a check-up for yourself.

2. Look for some relief from your caregiver duties; even if it is just for a day. This time away can be greatly beneficial to your well-being. Talk to the patient's doctor, social worker, or cancer care team about resources available in your community.

3. Consider joining a support group for caregivers. Call the American Cancer Society at 1-800-227-2345 for more information and referrals.

It isn't unusual for caregivers to have some of these problems for a short time but don't ignore the red flags or you run a higher chance of suffering your own physical and emotional distress. When caregivers don't attend to their own needs they can lose the ability to care for their loved one. Part of caring for someone else is caring for you first.

Asking for help is a good thing; don't wait too long. You should never feel inadequate or ashamed because you need a break from the day-to-day hardships, but as humans, we tend to feel both of those things.

Support programs for cancer patients and caregivers are available throughout the US. Locate your nearest group on-line and they can help you manage day-to-day and cope with physical and emotional changes. You trade information and experiences with other caregivers - all without leaving home.

It doesn't matter how strong you are, everyone can use support from time to time. Living with cancer, as a patient or as the caregiver, will be the most trying time of your life. It has some "ups" and it has a lot of "downs" but hopefully, everyone gets through it alive, healthy and happy. That's the end game. Some will make it, some will not.

Hard Choices

There will be many times through the cancer when you and the patient will not see eye-to-eye. This is normal in any full-time relationship but especially true here. The increased frustration levels often lead to disagreements about the decisions that need to be made and as it becomes harder for the patient to make the necessary decisions, we caregivers often become impatient. We want to continue to allow them to have full control over their destiny but when they struggle to do so, we tend to take over.

We begin by finishing their sentences and before long, by our nature; we begin to sub-consciously make decisions for the patient. Oftentimes we do this without considering their input or even asking for it. We think that the patient doesn't have the ability to make their own decisions so when they make the hardest one of all, we are shocked and sometimes, appalled at their choice.

One of the hardest things you will have to come to terms with is when your patient decides that enough is enough. They may eventually feel that the treatment to kill the cancer is no longer worth the cost to their quality of life.

My mother died of breast cancer on November 22, 2011. That was the second time in twenty-five years she'd been dealt that horrendous hand.

I know she wanted to fight it this time, too, but who were we kidding? We could all tell that she simply didn't have the strength to fight the cancer a second time.

I remember when my mom had breast cancer the first time. The treatment was barbaric. She had a full mastectomy and judging from my mother's experience, it is not something I ever want to go through.

The cancer had spread to her lungs before they found it the second time. She tried to fight for a couple of years but eventually she knew that the cancer would beat her. It had spread too fast for chemo-therapy and nothing they did stopped it. She made the decision to end her treatment and within a year, she passed away.

My sister and I spent those years taking care of her. We alternated our time at mom's house or we took her home with us for extended periods. We didn't want her to be alone through any of it. Kathie and I did the best we could to make the most of every minute we had left with our mother.

The three of us became very close during that time and I bonded with my mother on a whole new level; as her caregiver.

Growing up, my mom was a strong, vibrant red-head; kind to everyone around her. She took good care of us so it was important that Kathie and I be there for her and looking back, I can honestly say, I have no regrets.

My mother was a frail, sick woman when she came to Kathie and me with her decision to end cancer treatment. The three of us talked about it for a long time but in the end, it was her decision to make. We didn't like it, of course, because it meant that we would lose her but we supported her, in spite of our own feelings. After all, it wasn't our bodies ravaged by cancer drugs, it was hers.

We had her cremated, as per her request and Kathie and I share her remains; swapping her between our homes every couple of years. One day, we will spread her remains on Blood Mountain in North Georgia but until we are ready to do that, she will spend her days on the bookshelf in my office, with the photo of her and I sitting on top; or she will sit on Kathie's fireplace mantle watching the children fight and play. Either way, she is at peace.

Some cancers have cures and some do not. Some people will survive cancer and some, unfortunately, will die. The treatments can be deadly and when they stop working the patient is put on what is called a "maintenance dose." This smaller dose is designed to extend life for a short time. Sadly, it is no longer about finding a cure.

It is at this point that a great number of cancer patients will want to opt-out of treatment completely. It comes down to a choice; quality of life or quantity of life.

Some patients will want to let the cancer run its course and for the caregiver, this can be very upsetting. It would be common for the caregiver to feel anger at this decision because they may feel like they have invested all their time, energy, and resources into caring for a patient that is giving up now. They may ask themselves, "Why did I care for so long when they are just going to give up?"

Quitting was never an option and certainly not the outcome anyone had hoped for. The decision is an upsetting one for everyone, especially the patient. Without treatment, most cancer patients die in short order, so the decision to stop treatment is a personal one and ultimately, entirely up to the patient.

However, it is important that everyone be given an opportunity to discuss how they feel about the decision and to explain why they feel the way they do. There needs to be closure and it needs to end with the patient explaining life with cancer and what is it really like for them.

No one wants to die, but when you are that sick and there is no light at the end of the tunnel, sometimes death can be a welcome miracle.

It is best if you try to talk to the patient before any decision is made. Try to determine if the patient is of sound mind and body and can legally make this choice. If so, support their decision whether you agree with it or not. Assure them that you still love and care about them, no matter their choice. This is the same person you have always loved, so treat them the same as you always have.

For those who choose not to get cancer treatment at all, this can be very hard for the family and friends to understand. You may wonder why they would choose imminent death over fighting and your instinct will be to try to talk them into treatment. But there could be other reasons why it was necessary for the patient to make this terrible choice.

Maybe the person has additional health problems; diabetes or even a previous surgery could make cancer treatments harder or sometimes, impossible. Maybe they feel that because of the many risk factors and the daunting task in front of them, that maybe, it's just "their time" to go.

Some patients may have religious beliefs that could come into play. Or maybe the doctor has told the patient things that they haven't told you. Maybe there is no hope of a cure and the patient just wants to live out the rest of their life without the horrible side effects of chemo-therapy treatment. Maybe your patient is at peace with their choice and ready to move on. There are many reasons why people choose to stop fighting and we have to respect that choice.

Be sure to ask any questions you have of your loved one about why they made this choice. Explain to them that you want to put your own mind at peace, too. Now is the time to talk because as things progress, you may lose that luxury altogether.

If you have been around for the entire process of the cancer treatment, then you know what your patient has been going through; the deadly drugs, the fatigue, the constant pain. You have seen the exasperation when they look at rows of medicine bottles sitting next to the bed.

There have been so many drugs, too many appointments, and gallons of blood drawn from an exhausted body with no improvement in sight. Is it any wonder that they give up hope?

The choice to refuse treatment is the patient's but they may ask for your opinion and it's OK to tell the patient what you think, but that is all it is, your opinion.

But if you ask I am sure the patient will be glad to revisit all the treatment options with you, because two heads are always better than one. Maybe something was overlooked and there really is another option or maybe they just need you to see what is really going on through their eyes,

For the terminally ill patient, their reasons are sound. They have been in pain for so long, sick for as long as they can remember and the growing distress watching their body continuously deteriorate.

They have lost control of their lives. Everything from paying the bills to basic hygiene is being handled through other people. This can be soul-crushing to the patient and because they see no end to it at all, they make their choice.

The last and final thing that they have control of is when and where they actually "check-out." The way they see it is simple: either cancer controls the process of death or they control it. With that luxury, the terminally ill patient can make assured that final arrangements are made and that everything is the way they want it to be. Who can blame them for wanting to go out on their own terms? They don't want cancer dictating the way.

You can take comfort in knowing that you have done the best that you could possibly do. You gave them comfort through it all so give them comfort once again. Tell them something like, "I am pleased that you shared your feelings with me and I promise to do everything I can to support your choice. I will be with you through it all; until the very end." This will give them peace of mind to know that they will not be alone.

This may be one of those times where you don't agree with the decision made but bear in mind; it is not your decision to make. Don't let the patient's choice to stop fighting cancer change your relationship. Don't clam up or become aloof. You are still a team and it will give the patient tremendous peace of mind to know that you are there.

Once the decision to stop treatment has been made by the patient there needs to be a conversation with the doctor. He can clarify whether there is hope for a positive outcome or is the end inevitable.

Hopefully, after speaking with the doctor, the patient will want to continue living. Sometimes a heart-to-heart talk with the doctor can provide hope for a miracle and the desire to carry on in the fight.

Ask the doctor if there is any reason to continue treatment. Be blunt with him and force him to answer direct questions. I have found that doctors like to be selective in their distribution of information and if you don't ask the question in the right way, they will be evasive. You have to ask something like this. "Is there any chance that I will survive this cancer? How long do I have to live?"

If talking with the doctor didn't change the patients mind and they still refuse future treatments; don't be upset. Don't get into an argument with them. This is not about you or anyone else. It is solely about the patient and their desire to continue. Try to see it from their point of view, and continue to offer your support and love.

It is hard to know how long a person who refuses treatment will survive, but even those at the end of their battle with cancer may still want some additional care. For them, there is Hospice Care.

Hospice workers give supportive care to control symptoms and to keep the patient as comfortable as possible while the cancer runs its course. They also help the family make the most of the time they have left and help to prepare for the inevitable. This care will be needed even more as the patient's condition worsens and the family and loved ones can no longer manage without the professional help.

It takes a very special person to be a Hospice Nurse. I have met many of them in my lifetime and they are really angels disguised as people. They never know the patients for very long but in the short time that they do know them, they make them feel like they are the most important. It seems appropriate that they are the last line of defense for the patient battling cancer. They have a way of calming everyone when they need calming the most, at the very end.

Their job is not to give cancer treatment, their job is to do nothing more than keep the patient comfortable and as pain-free as possible. They will talk the patient and the family through the process of dying and when the time finally comes, they will handle everything.

Some patients will want to talk about death and dying and some will not. Most people find the subject unpleasant because they don't know what to say or how to approach the dying cancer patient.

Many patients worry about their will because most of us are woefully unprepared in that area. If you haven't already made your final arrangements, there is no time for delay. The Hospice workers can guide you and the person with cancer through things like living wills and advance directives but it is best to have a professional take care of any final arrangements.

It is natural for a dying patient to ask the questions, "What will happen when I'm actually dying?" or "Will I feel anything when my time comes?" Hospice can answer questions about the process of the body dying but no one really knows what happens when the soul dies. All we can do is be reassuring. Let the patient know that they are not alone.

Hospice staff members are trained and observant. They are used to answering tough questions, and they are skilled in doing it in a supportive, caring manner. Hospice workers are not only experts; they are compassionate, caring people who will take the best care possible of your loved one.

You have been taking care of this person for months or years but these last few weeks of the cancer will be the hardest for you emotionally. It is so heartbreaking to watch someone you love go through this process of dying.

You'll want to hang on to the memory of who they were but seeing them like this will stick with you for a lifetime.

All you can do now is be there, no matter how hard it may be. Your time as a caregiver is not over yet and it's still important to be there right to the end.

You are the one who is in sync with the patient and you are the one they will want beside them. Just stay close and show how much you care with a smile or gentle touch.

It is time for courage; for the patient, for you and for everyone who will be hurt by this loss. If you show strength, the rest will show strength and the patient will feel the strength that only his family can provide for him. This should be a peaceful time. No drama, just calm.

All you can do now is hold your loved one's hand and tell them how much they mean to you. It is OK to cry together and talk about the sadness and share old memories. Be engaged in these last moments because they really are the last ones you will have with your loved one.

There are no magic words to say to a person dying of cancer. Often, your presence and your loving heart is all they require at this final stage of their life. Be there. You deserve to be.

Cancer and the Marriage

One thing we have barely touched on is the devastating effect that cancer has on a marriage. According to a study done by Dr. Marc Chamberlain, a Seattle oncologist, the over-all rate of divorce when a cancer diagnosis is received is about 12% in a sampling of 515 patients. Living through it myself, I am actually surprised that the number is not much higher.

The emotional and physical stress that a marriage endures when one of the partners has cancer can be intense and everlasting. It is during this time that the relationship experiences it's most bi-polar range of behavior and emotions. Couples are forced to confront the changing roles and responsibilities as the healthy partner must step-up to take over the tasks that the patient previously handled.

For the caregiver, the healthy partner, it can be overwhelming to suddenly be thrust into this ever-growing role. You are now "everything to everyone" and this can be terrifying, to say the least.

The transition is difficult for everyone in the family as new feelings of fear, resentment, anger, anxiety and grief may arise. When financial issues surface, and they so often do, piled on top of household chores or childcare tasks; it can become more than the healthy spouse can handle.

If your marriage is strong, as many are, you will come out the other side, scarred but maybe still together. If your marriage was stressed before the cancer, you will need extra help to make it through. But be strong. Anything worth having is worth fighting for.

How a couple relates to one another as they handle each cancer crisis will have a tremendous impact on their relationship later on.

Though Marcus lost Karen to her cancer and Beatrix lost Carlos to his, Lola and John were able to keep their marriage together - when all the odds were against them. They lost nearly everything they owned including their dignity but they were determined to keep their family together. It was all they had left.

Unfortunately, not everyone enjoys the same outcome.

Jeannie and Peter

Hello! My name is Jeannie. I have been a cancer patient for four years now. I am getting treatment but my battle with cancer rages on. I am doing OK now but in the beginning, I did everything wrong.

I was determined that I would handle this on my own. I was not going to let cancer become a big deal in our lives. I knew I was strong and I thought, "I can do this myself." I was naive.

I remember thinking, "What are a few cancer treatments? I can squeeze them into my busy days. I don't need anyone's help." I was certain that no one would even notice that I had cancer. Life would go on as it always had. That was the plan, anyway.

Well things didn't exactly turn out that way and my words would come back to haunt me.

Things looked hopeful in the beginning and I was certain of a quick recovery but after a year of nothing but setbacks, I was beginning to lose my patience. Worse, my husband, Peter, was beginning to lose patience with me.

He has been a great caregiver from day one and I don't think I would have gotten this far without him. Unfortunately, the toll it has taken on him is undeniable. He is angry most of the time, quick to temper, then quick to apologize. I can't remember the last time I saw him excited about anything or even remotely happy.

I do what I can to take some stress off of him but with my illness; it just never seems like enough. He carries the weight of everything and as much as I hate to admit it, I see it in his face. He is starting to resent me.

He takes care of the shopping and the errands because the possibility of germ exposure is too great; and he takes our child wherever she needs to be.

He won't ask for help because that is not the "manly" thing to do but then does nothing but complain about how stressful and lonely his life has become. He blames my illness for us having no social life and he certainly blames me for the loss of our intimate life. He says he wants time for himself but what he really means is - time away from me.

He has become bitter and he blames me for getting cancer. He reminds me all the time about how far along we would have been if I had not gotten sick. As if reminding me was going to change anything. "It's not your fault." he says. But he really doesn't believe that.

Peter's life was stolen from him, too. The day they diagnosed me was the beginning of the end.

We had a promising future on the horizon but when I got sick that all but evaporated. I had to stop working and that put the entire burden on Peter.

Soon enough, Peter was forced to take a leave from work to take care of me and that forced us to live off of our savings and retirement. Once my Social Security Disability came in and Peter saw that it was enough to take care of us and that we didn't need him to be anything other than my caregiver, he began to feel like less of a man.

He felt like he was living off his sick wife's government check. He would forget to see how much he was helping me. He just wanted his pity-party.

I would tell him to go out with his friends. I suggested that he return to the gym or find a hobby. I told him that he didn't have to sit at home all the time just because I was sick.

For the first few years he didn't take me up on it, but after some time he began to go out. Before long, he was going out routinely and it seemed like he was moving on with his life without me. That was when we really began to drift apart. I pushed him to go out and in doing so, I pushed him away.

Peter began to see that there was still a world outside of our cancer-ridden home and he liked it out there.

I knew how hard life had been for Peter since I became ill and I knew what he had hoped his life would be by now and the two lives didn't reconcile. I should have seen his affair coming and in hind-sight, I suppose I did, but I let it happen anyway.

I am angry at him for not being strong enough to make it to the end with me. I thought he was a bigger man than that. We have known each other for most of our lives and yet, when I needed him, he couldn't handle it.

I don't blame him for how he feels because his life was turned upside down by my illness, too. But right now, our marriage is all about resentment. I love my husband but I'm starting to feel like I should force him to move out so he can rebuild what is left of his life.

He has a right to find happiness, enjoy his life and since his heart is not in it anymore, I would rather he not be around.

We are separated now. I have moved in with my sister and our adult daughter moves between Peter and me.

There isn't a day that goes by that I don't cry about that; but what can I do about it? Maybe Peter and I would have made it had I not gotten sick but we will never know. I always thought we had a strong marriage but in the end, it wasn't strong enough. Cancer killed it.

Jeannie

Stanley and Gloria

I love my wife, Gloria, now more than ever. I have seen strength in her that I have never seen before. Her cancer diagnosis was a devastating blow to our family and even though her prognosis is good for the moment, cancer may still cost us our marriage.

My name is Stanley and I think my wife would agree with me when I say that we had an excellent marriage before her cancer.

We did quite well over the years. We saved money and my business was successful. We could afford a good lifestyle. Gloria was able to stay at home to raise our children and now they are in college; far away from the cancer.

Every day is a new crisis. Every day brings new pain and now all she can tell me is that I "can't understand." I try to sympathize, empathize, and comfort her in any way I know how. I listen to her and cry with her and now she has the audacity to say that I don't understand.

I have walked through hell and back for this woman. I have cleaned up after her and kept her alive when she wanted to die. I have been there for every single minute of her cancer but now she feels that her having cancer and surviving; somehow places her above me in some way. It is almost a spiritual thing with her. She looks down on the rest of us now because we haven't had cancer. In a sick sort of way, she feels superior.

She has conveniently forgotten who wiped her chin and fed her meals, flushed her lines and dressed bandages? Did she forget who sat for many hundreds of hours in the hard, back-killing chairs at the cancer ward.....for her? Did she forget who did everything while she laid in bed for the first two years recovering, doped up on medication and unaware of anything going on around her?

It seemed to me that Gloria had a totally different recollection of what happened than I did. She looks back on it and remembers me nagging her with my constant, "Take your medication," or "It is time to leave for your appointment." The things I did out of love, she found bothersome.

It was difficult at times to get her to do what she was supposed to do. She was always argumentative with me and she really believed that her stress didn't come from the cancer, but from me always hovering over her.

She will always be the number one priority in my life but I've backed off because she makes me feel inferior and no longer useful.

I had always heard that cancer patients and cancer survivors were forever changed. I believe it now. I have experienced it myself. They will never look at the world or the people around them the same again, as Gloria puts it, "I have looked death in the face and death looked back."

Cancer really does try to kill everything around it and sometimes, it succeeds. It will take my wife someday but it might as well have taken her the moment we learned of her cancer. We have not been the same since that day.

She now sees me through what she calls her "post-cancer" eyes. She says that having cancer has forced her to re-access our marriage and she didn't like what she saw. She said she wasn't sure she wanted to be married any longer.

She said that facing death made her realize that she had not accomplished much in her life and

I was tying her down. There were things she wanted to do before cancer defeated her.

I'm in counseling to get the help that I need and she is in counseling to deal with the issues that come with chemo, cancer, and life-changes. We both attend a group therapy and I will always be there for her.

She says that she will never leave me. "Till death do us part" she reminds me. But I can see that she has checked out of the marriage in more ways than one. Honestly, so have I.

I still love my wife and my family dearly. I hate cancer and what it has done to all of us.

Stanley

These are just two stories out of untold numbers just like them.

Marriage doesn't usually fair well when cancer is involved. The stresses are so high that most people crack at some point and for a wide range of reasons. Don't let your marriage be a casualty of your war with cancer.

In this battle, you will have to fight like you have never fought before and believe me when I say, you will want to quit, but don't. Remember that your spouse is still the same person you fell in love with and the love you shared so deeply is what will keep you together now. It will be a hard fought victory but the prize is so worth it.

Dear Friends and Family

This section is provided as a guide for family and friends. Print it out for anyone who plans to spend time with the patient. This recap of the things we touched on in previous chapters is condensed into a bulleted list for easy reference. With this in hand, you will know that everyone is on the same page because they have the guidelines at their fingertips

Feel free to use this as a starting point and revise as needed to fit your situation. The more information everyone has, the better off you will be.

To our Dear Family and Friends

Remember to:

1. Talk when talking is warranted but be OK
with silence, too. The silence may help the patient
focus their thoughts. Talking because you are
nervous can be irritating to anyone but especially a
sick person. Silence can be comforting and allows
time for the patient to ponder on their thoughts and
feelings.

2. Maintain eye contact with the patient
when talking. This gives a sense that you are
present and paying attention.

3. Touching, smiling, and warm words can
brighten the life of a cancer patient. So often they
are met with unpleasant news. Your cheerfulness
can turn their sadness into joy within moments.

4. Ask questions and listen but try not to offer advice on subjects you don't know about personally. If you are not in their shoes, it will come across as condescending if you try to offer them advice.

5. Talk about things unrelated to cancer. Cancer patients don't always want to talk about their illness. They don't want to be identified as "the cancer patient." Joking, laughter and talking about other things are welcome distractions.

6. Maintain routine, if possible, and try to do the things you used to do. If you used to play cards – play cards now! If you used to go to the movies together – keep going to movies or watch movies together at home. Use sound judgment in determining your loved one's energy level and make certain that they take breaks. Be conscious of their cancer, but don't be overprotective. Keep

urging the patient to do things with you and other people.

7. Visit often but for those who can't visit, write, email, or call. This will help keep the patient's mood buoyant. Cancer can be very lonely and isolating and sometimes the unexpected call from someone who cares is all it takes to cheer up a dark day. Your love and concern is always important and appreciated.

8. Just be yourself. Try not to worry about whether you are doing things the right way. Let your words and your actions come from your heart. Your compassion and genuine caring are the most important things you can express right now.

9. Show understanding but remember; you don't have to tolerate abusive behavior just because someone is ill.

10. Don't take things too personally. All emotions are on the table when dealing with a cancer patient. Expect the person with cancer to have good days and bad days. Keep your relationship as normal and balanced as possible. Greater patience and compassion are called for during these times and we have to respect the feelings of everyone involved.

11. Never go around someone with cancer if you are sick, have a fever or any other signs of infection. The cancer patient is very susceptible to sickness as their immune system may not be at 100%. Keep your colds and germs at home. Visit when you are well.

It's human nature to maintain a distance from someone when they become ill. Cancer can force us to look at our own fears about illness, weakness, or our own mortality. This may make us reluctant to interact with a cancer patient. But isolation is never healthy for someone with cancer or their caregiver. Make the effort to reach out to your loved one or friend.

The person with cancer may find it hard to ask for help or may be worried about appearing weak or vulnerable.

Cancer patients really don't want to hear, "You're so brave," or "You're so strong." These types of phrases, as simple as they seem to most, will actually place a lot of pressure on the patient to act strong when they may not feel up to it.

Please, don't forget the caregiver. They will also need help and support. The caregiver can become isolated and stressed, too. Check in to see how they are doing and offer assistance where you can.

Here are some ideas that you can utilize in order to make things easier for the caregiver:

1. Prepare a meal. Arrange a schedule for others to do the same.

2. Offer to help with child care if the caregiver has children.

3. Offer to take the patient to and from appointments.

4. Run errands.

5. Take over being the caregiver for a day. They will need the break.

6. Coordinate visits and solicit others to send cards, flowers, or gifts to the patient and the caregiver.

7. A contribution to a related charity in the name of the patient is a great way to honor them during this time.

8. When they have unanswered questions, offer to do the research for them.

9. If the patient is healthy enough and the caregiver agrees, plan a party to celebrate the end of treatment and hopefully their remission.

10. Always wear a bright, cheerful smile when you visit. A Smile is contagious.

Always remember that when dealing with a cancer patient, communication is the key to success. You can be most helpful to the patient by equipping yourself with the knowledge of how best to care for them. This will give you confidence in your abilities and make you more comfortable with everything that is taking place. Be a good friend. Be informed.

My Story

Cancer has taken my family on its tumultuous ride as well and so far, we have managed to survive; but not without our share of scars. As my husband's caregiver, I can honestly say that this has been the hardest years of my life. Not only have they been physically draining but the emotional roller-coaster ride has been exhausting.

I know the isolation that comes with being a caregiver. My husband slept for nearly two years. But I let him do it because I read that the body fights cancer faster while sleeping than when awake.[3] Knowing that, however, didn't change how it made me feel. I not only had to keep people

---

3

http://www.dailymail.co.uk/health/artic
le-90598/What-happens-body-youre-
asleep.html

out of the home because of his defenseless immune system but the loneliness inside the home was suffocating, too. After a couple of years of this, I succumbed to Caregiver Depression.

My husband's mother, Barbara was a tremendous help but his constant grouchiness soon drove her to "help from a distance." Who could blame her? He was awful to her when he felt bad. There were times when I wished that I could have faded into the background, too.

I tried too hard to do everything myself without involving anyone else. Looking back on it now, I see that I could've done a few things differently but as my eldest daughter is so fond of telling me, "Could've, would've, should've, Mom."

My biggest regret through it all is that I sheltered our children from the horrors of their father's cancer.

Our three oldest daughters were living on their own while our son was in his junior year of high school. They were all so involved with their own lives that it was easy to allow them to remain oblivious, but in doing that, I cut off an entire wing of my support system.

I didn't tell them what I was going through, or how close we came to losing him, so they were confused when I would call them out of the blue. I thought I was protecting them but in the end, all I did was shut them out of something very important, albeit tragic, that was happening to our family. I wish I hadn't done that.

My advice to anyone with children; make them a part of as much as you can. They need to know what is going on because knowledge is power to them, too. It will give them more comfort to be informed than it will to let their imaginations do the explaining for you.

Like many people before us, with us and coming after us, cancer has devastated so much of our lives. My husband and I owned two businesses when cancer came knocking on our door and today we are homebodies, no longer business owners.

He is confined to bed a great deal and when I am not taking care of him, I write as much as I can. It is intellectually stimulating for me and provides me a vehicle for venting my stress. Yes, there may a book or two of rantings hidden away, never to be published but there are plenty more that I will publish. If I had to find a bright side to all of this, it would that. My husband's cancer turned me into a writer and I love that new part of my life.

That being said, we share the same experiences of hardship and sacrifice that so many other cancer patients and caregivers experience. We have and still are walking alongside you.

Cancer patients feel as if they have been delivered a death sentence. They completely stop thinking about life and quit doing the things they used to enjoy. Their future has been stolen from them and, for some; they will never get it back.

Don't expect the cancer patient or the caregiver to be brave all the time. It's just not possible. In the words of my dear, loving and warm-hearted husband, "No one really understands the profound grief that you feel when you get a cancer diagnosis." He goes on to explain that, "Cancer stole my health and my life. I have lost almost everything because of it. I hate Cancer. It really does suck."

Until the patient begins to see progress in treatment, they feel no real optimism about the future. They feel an absolute loss of will to participate in life. I have seen this so many times. I have seen it in my husband.

This is where family and friends are so important. You can play an important role by simply being there. The building of trust, the continued encouragement, and a lot of compassion is what it takes to be a good caregiver.

As much as I would like to say that this book will have no readers, I am afraid that is likely not the case. The ranks of caregivers are growing every day. Those of us who have been through it need to help the newly diagnosed as they begin their terrifying walk with cancer. I hope this book will serve in that capacity for the millions of people who are just like me.

Thank you for reading. Be strong, be steadfast and remember; YOU are not alone.

Additional Resources

There are many sources of support for people facing cancer and those caring for cancer patients. These include visitation programs like the American Cancer Society Reach To Recovery® program (for women with breast cancer), ostomy education (for patients with stomas on the belly), and laryngectomy clubs (for those who have lost their natural voice because of cancer surgery).

The American Cancer Society I Can Cope® program is another good source of support and information. It can help you learn more about cancer diagnosis, treatment, side effects, nutrition, and other topics of interest to people with cancer and those close to them.[2]

2

[http://www.cancer.org/treatment/suppor
tprogramsservices/onlinecommunities/par
ticipateinacancereducationclass/icancop

It's hard to watch as a loved one suffers through the effects of cancer treatment. If you need help coping with your distress in regards to their illness, know that help is readily available.

The Social Services department of the Cancer Center or hospital or even your doctor's office may be able to help you or direct you to someone who can help you. They may be able to suggest support groups in your area for friends and families of cancer patients. Sometimes the chaplain at the hospital or your own clergy can help. Asking other cancer patients and their caregivers who they see for counseling is a great way to get additional support. Don't feel selfish that you may need support too. As the caregiver, know that by helping yourself you will be able to help your loved one.

eonline/index]

The ACS has valuable information, just for the asking. You can order free copies of these materials by calling the toll-free number of the American Cancer Society at 1-800-227-2345, or you can read them online at www.cancer.org.

Some of the subjects are as follows:

1. More on Relating to People with Cancer

2. When Someone You Know Has Cancer (also in Spanish)

3. When Someone You Work With Has Cancer (also in Spanish)

4. How to Be a Friend to Someone With Cancer

5. Learn More About Cancer and What to Expect

6.   After Diagnosis: A Guide for Patients and Families (also in Spanish)

7.   Coping with Cancer in Everyday Life (also in Spanish)

8.   What You Need to Know as a Cancer Caregiver

9.   What It Takes to Be a Caregiver

10. Caring for the Patient with Cancer at Home: A Guide for Patients and Families (also in Spanish)

11. Advanced Cancer (also in Spanish)

12. Advance Directives

13. Nearing the End of Life (also in Spanish)

14. Hospice Care

Along with the American Cancer Society, there are many other valuable resources for information and support. Check out the following:

CancerCare (one word) offers free professional support services to anyone affected by cancer, including things like telephone counseling, on-line support groups, workshops, and publications. You can reach them at:

Toll-free number: 1-800-813-4673

Website: www.cancercare.org

The Cancer Support Community has support groups for patients, caregivers, and loved ones, as well as open discussion groups that are available 24/7; all are password protected and led by trained professionals. You can reach them at:

Toll-free number: 1-888-793-9355

Website: www.cancersupportcommunity.org

The Family Caregiver Alliance
(FCA)/National Center on Caregiving provides
information for caregivers such as guidelines for
better communication, decision making, and how
to hold a family meeting, as well as free on-line
workshops and support groups. They can be
reached at:

Toll-free number: 1-800-445-8106

Website: www.caregiver.org

The National Cancer Institute (NCI) has up-
to-date information on cancer and many cancer-
related topics, including caregiving. Reach them
at:

Toll-free number: 1-800 422-6237 (1-800-4-CANCER) or for TTY call: 1-800-332-8615

Website: www.cancer.gov

Disclaimer: Inclusion on this does not mean that I, as the author, endorse these organizations, but I do believe they are invaluable for their information. My advice for you is to read everything from every source about cancer and dealing with cancer and then you will be better informed on what to do and how to get help.

Additional Resources

A Note from the Author

Dear Reader,

Before I began writing this book I felt as if I was totally alone in dealing with my husband's cancer. And I am certain that you felt the same way or you wouldn't have reached for this particular book.

After writing it, thus reliving it, I realized that there were things I did right and things I did wrong. I made many of the classic mistakes but I know in my heart that I did the best I could.

My husband is a fighter. He is strong and brave. He is like every other cancer patients with a strength and courage that many of us will never know. We only watch from the outside as they wage a battle for their lives on the inside.

Caregivers are the angels that wrap their wings around the cancer stricken soul. They nurse the body and the mind of the patient and without the caregiver, the patient would be lost.

Like me, you will learn many things through your walk with cancer. Some of them; you will learn the hard way; others will come easier.

I want to leave you with one last thing that I have personally come to understand through it all. I realize now that I am stronger than I ever knew, more determined than I have ever been and steadfast in my belief that cancer will not kill my husband and it will not kill me. We will fight it and we will win.

I want us all to be able to say the same words, "Cancer, You Lose!"
Kimberly Bratton

A Note From the Author